The History of Witchcraft

Traditions, Practices and the Trials of Witches, Wizards and Warlocks. Spells, Rites and Rituals, Sorcery and Magic from Ancient Times to Modern Day Wicca and Neo-Paganism

DELORES E. WREN

Copyright © 2023 by Delores E. Wren. All rights reserved.

The content contained within this book may not be reproduced, duplicated, or transmitted without direct written permission from the author or the publisher. This book is copyright protected. It is only for personal use. You cannot amend, distribute, sell, use any part or the content within this book, without the consent of the author or publisher.

This publication endeavours to provide accurate and authoritative information in regard to the subject covered. While the publisher and author have used their best efforts in preparing this book, they make no representations or warranties with respect to the accuracy or completeness of the contents of this book. All effort has been executed to present accurate, reliable, complete information.

Please note the information contained within this document is for educational and entertainment purposes only. The content within this book has been derived from various sources and every effort has been used to state such sources.

1st edition 2023

Cover by RGRAPHIC

Fortune Telling by Cards Book

As a way of saying thank you for your purchase, there is an additional book which I have written called "Fortune Telling by Cards". I am making the book available free to my readers. It is not available anywhere else. Fortune telling by cards, or cartomancy, is a form of fortune telling or divination that involves using standard playing cards used to gain insight into the past, present, or future.

While some people believe in the power of divination, through playing cards or otherwise, others are more sceptical. Some view it as a form of entertainment or a tool for self-reflection, while others believe the insights gained through divination can be used to make positive changes in their life. Regardless of these beliefs, both the history of playing cards and their practical use in divination is a fascinating subject that continues to capture the imagination of many people today. This book may just surprise you.

To download, please go to:

https://amitylifebooks.com/deloreswren

Table of Contents

Introduction	7
Chapter 1: What Is Witchcraft?	11
Chapter 2: Famous Witches	25
Chapter 3: Witchcraft Practices	37
Chapter 4: The Origin and Evolution of Witchcraft	77
Chapter 5: The Spread of Witchcraft Across the Globe	103
Chapter 6: Witch Hunts Throughout History	121
Chapter 7: The Witch Trials in Europe	145
Chapter 8: The Witch Trials in North America	173
Chapter 9: The History of Witchcraft in Russia	185
Chapter 10: Witches in the Arts, Myths and Legends	199
Chapter 11: Modern Day Witch Hunts	215
Chapter 12: Modern Witchcraft Today	227
Conclusion	237

Introduction

"Most books on witchcraft will tell you that witches work naked. This is because most books on witchcraft are written by men." — *Neil Gaiman*[1]

Witchcraft has existed for centuries, dating back to ancient times, and is present in cultures around the world today. The term originated in the late Middle Ages and the beginning of Modernity in Europe, when people were accused of attacking their own community through harmful magic and invoking supernatural powers associated with evil. These people were mostly women and the poor. Magical thinking provided them with a system of ideas to understand the world that surrounded them, and to cover essential needs that the social system could not provide.

There was widespread belief in witchcraft, and its practice, as the embodiment of evil. From the simple peasant through to members of the higher echelons of society, people would turn to *cunning folk* or folk healers to protect themselves from its evils.

Suspected witches have been persecuted throughout history. Believers, practitioners and followers of witchcraft were intimidated, banished from their communities, attacked, and even killed. Those suspected of witchcraft could also be prosecuted according to the laws that established witchcraft as a crime against God and the social order. A judicial inquiry,

---
[1] English author

included torture would ensue. If the accused were found guilty, they received terrible punishment, including death.

Today, witchcraft is still practiced by people around the world. Though often maligned and misunderstood, it continues to be a powerful and influential force in many cultures, manifesting itself through traditional rituals and spells, as well as modern spiritual practices like Wicca or Neo-paganism. Whether viewed as an ancient art, a form of harmful evil, or a spiritual path to connect with the divine, witchcraft remains an enduring part of human history and culture.

Is it true that we have truly evolved?

Have we really left behind irrational fears that once led to the hunting and execution of people?

What is the purpose of witchcraft today, when science and technology seem to have the answers to all our questions?

The intention of this book is to explore the different conceptions of witchcraft and the social and cultural context of changes in those conceptions throughout history. There are common elements that are intrinsic characteristics of human nature. However, there are always contextual circumstances that can help to understand why some ideas, fears, and needs are socially built with particular nuances. In this sense, we shall explore the similarities and differences between Europe and the countries influenced by its culture, and other continents that followed a different path. Then, together, we shall try to understand how the evolution of the Western conception of witchcraft is encompassed with the economic, social, political, and intellectual evolution of humankind's history.

Witchcraft has called upon the attention of scholars of different fields, and for a better understanding, it is essential to cover this issue through comparative and interdisciplinary studies. This includes a historical reconstruction of the processes and facts, a description of cultural aspects, and the theoretical framework to approach social phenomena. Then, the anthropological, sociological, and historical approaches assist in the appropriate treatment of the issue. Without delving into theoretical explanations, these sciences provide concepts to overcome the simple thinking that can lead to misjudgement or fall into prejudices.

Although this book retrieves contributions from different fields, scholarly research might not be enough. Witchcraft has developed at the back, and sometimes against, the truths of scientific knowledge. Hence, witchcraft needs to be treated, explained, and understood from a holistic approach. Therefore, this book collects several theoretical approaches but also gathers the insights of people specialised in this issue, sometimes outside the boundaries of scientific knowledge. Witchcraft has always been an alternative way to understand life, and everything that happens on earth, and anywhere else. A real interest in witchcraft implies venturing into the unknown, beyond reason and rational thought.

Witchcraft has been present in human history, from the beginning of times and despite the progress of scientific knowledge. The attraction for the mysterious, of the inexplicable, for the desire to anticipate and control fate, as well as the desire for power over the overwhelming nature and life, are the conditions that make witchcraft as a force today, as in the past.

Who we are as humankind in the present is somehow the result of everything that preceded us in the past. This is the adventure of learning about a hidden side of our humanity, with its shadow and light, and with all its fears and hopes.

Chapter 1: What Is Witchcraft?

Human nature seeks understanding. It does not withstand the unpredictable, the incomprehensible, and everything that falls out of its control. Sometimes, the answers found are not enough. There are matters that are beyond human comprehension and questions that remain unsolved. Furthermore, some of the answers are unbearable for human understanding.

The mysterious and supernatural have always been a matter of attention for cultures around the world. From ancient times, humankind has searched for all means to acquire the power to control natural forces and destiny, to win the battle over everything that causes pain or frustration, and to defeat illness and death.

Is witchcraft one of those means?

To start, it is difficult to arrive at a unified conception of what the word means. If we start with the dictionary definition, we find that there is more than one, and despite that they are all related, there are significant differences among them. According to one Merriam-Webster (n.d.) dictionary edition, witchcraft is "the use of sorcery or magic" but also—within the same definition: "communication with the devil or with a familiar" (Merriam-Webster, 2022). There is another definition to consider: "rituals and practices that incorporate beliefs in magic and that are associated especially with neo-pagan traditions and religions (such as Wicca)".

According to the Britannica Encyclopaedia, witchcraft has different significance due to historical and cultural frames. In general, it refers to the invocation of supernatural powers intending to dominate something or someone. The term has also been associated with practices of sorcery, magic, cannibalism, and rituals invoking the Devil or other demons, particularly in Western culture (Burton Russell, 2022).

Figure 1: This illustration captures the mystical practices associated with witchcraft and sorcery. An illustration from "The History of Witches and Wizards" (1720). The scene shows the Devil bestowing wax dolls upon a group of witches. Public domain, via Wikimedia Commons (https://commons.wikimedia.org/wiki/File:Agnes_Sampson_and_witc hes_with_devil.jpg)

The term "witchcraft" is used by many anthropologists, after the study of different languages and cultures, to refer to, quite simply, as "practices carried out by witches". The term "witch" being defined, in this example as "any person, male or female, believed to have caused the misfortune of others through psychic, magical, or other occult power" (Priest, 2012). According to the same author, there are other types of people who use these practices to fight evil that are, however, socially approved.

The concept of witchcraft is complex, and its meaning will be discussed and clarified throughout the following pages. Controversies, questions and debate will undoubtedly remain. Defining witchcraft presents a challenge because it underlines other words and practices that overlap with other concepts and beliefs such as magic, folklore and religion.

Where Does the Word Come From?

For this, we will need to look at another definition. According to the Britannica Encyclopaedia, the term witchcraft has at least three different connotations in the modern English language: "the practice of magic or sorcery worldwide; the beliefs associated with the Western witch hunts of the 14th to the 18th century; and varieties of the modern movement called Wicca" (Burton Russell, 2022).

The word *"wikka"* can be traced to an old English word, *wiccecraeft,* that alludes to ancient Anglo-Saxon practices between the 5th and the 11th century. According to different archaeological evidence and anthropological interpretation, many of these practices consisted mostly of the use of enchantments, amulets, and herbal mixtures to heal illness.

After the Christianisation of England, all these practices were categorised as witchcraft.

The English term *wiccecraeft* is composed of two others: *wicca*-males and *wicce*-female. *Wicca* and *wicce* were those who practiced sorcery—the use of power gained from the help or control of evil spirits especially for divining (Merriam-Webster, n.d.). The second term, *craeft*, meaning craft.

In early modern Europe, witches were defined by Jean Bodin, a demonology and political theorist, in this way: "A witch is one who knowingly tries to accomplish something by diabolical means" (Lynn, 2018).

Historically, an accurate definition was essential since it had not only social effects, but dire consequences. In the 14th century, the witch hunts had begun. There were conditions to determine what a witch was.

Where Did Witchcraft Start?

Robert Priest (2012) affirms that the polysemy of the word witchcraft, due to cultural nuances, presents challenges in delimiting the concept. In other languages, the equivalents for the term mean different things and cannot be translated from one unto another. The words *hexerei*, in German, *stregoneria* in Italian, and *brujería* in Spanish cannot be considered synonyms.

As mentioned, the word witchcraft can be traced to Anglo-Saxon traditions: "As early as the 7th century, Theodore of Tarsus imposed penances upon magicians and enchanters, and the laws, from Alfred on, abound with mentions of witchcraft" (Notestein, 2014).

In early times, the term alluded to supernatural powers obtained with the help of demons, but there was no mention of the Devil's worshippers or human relationships with evil creatures (Notestein, 2014). According to Notestein's (2014) research, the concept was influenced by the stories introduced by the Byzantine Empire during the 7th century. However, the ideas about witchcraft relating to Sabbath and pacts with the Devil appeared in Europe in the 14th century. Later, the concept of witchcraft was formalised and shaped by the law. Subsequently, it was then considered a crime.

Magic beliefs were very common in Europe during the Middle Ages, and were mostly associated with healing since there were no other means of access to medicine. For the vernacular conceptions, "the witch was essential as a healer and unbewitcher in a society that had little access to, and much distrust of, formal medicine. Yet witches were also feared for their supernatural powers and their reputed ability to do harm" (Magliocco, 2018). Even though Magliocco's studies are centred in Italy, her arguments can explain the relationship between the uses and social role of magic in Europe. Peasants and people from lower social levels relied on folk healers to treat their illnesses. These healers knew the properties of natural herbs and how to use them to alleviate illness and disease. Consequently, it should be seen that magic was a protective strategy for the poorest.

Magliocco (2018) also describes the folkloric witch, a supernatural and legendary figure with supernatural powers, usually applied with negative connotations. This figure is not a healing character. This character has the ability and the power to fly, transform into an animal, influence people's lives, and hurt them. This figure of the folkloric witch condenses the most common fears of people.

Other practices that can be placed under the concept of folklore—even being considered magical—are syncretised practices that invoke any supernatural force to obtain certain goals, not necessarily constrained in any religious system, or dedicated to a specific divinity or evil entity (Folk magic and witchcraft | What's the difference, 2016).

Much scholarly research has achieved the conclusion that witchcraft is related to the mythical explanation of misfortune (Singh, 2020). According to these theories, witchcraft relies on the popular belief that the witch has the power to cause harm, for instance, the evil eye. This phenomenon is a widespread belief that implies: "the often inadvertent *jettatura* or *malocchio* (evil eye) to more intentional magical attacks, known as *attaccatura* (attachment), *fascino* or *legatura* (binding), and *fattura* (fixing)" (Magliocco, 2018). However, Singh (2020) affirms that this conception excludes many features of witchcraft and that misfortune is also attributed to other entities that exist outside its boundaries—evil spirits and other malign entities.

Professor Ronald Hutton studied witchcraft in depth. Besides tracing its origins to Anglo-Saxon tradition, he defines five main characteristics that should be considered when speaking about witchcraft. The first characteristic that he finds to define witches is the common belief that there are people who have the power to cause pain to others, and this belief can be explained by the human incapability to cope with random chances (Hutton, 2017).

Besides this characteristic, Hutton also considered that witches were an internal threat to the community rather than a danger coming from the outside. In the Middle Ages in Europe, the victims of witches were rarely strangers, and witchcraft was a different phenomenon from using magic to fight against other villages. Then, the third characteristic of witchcraft combines two types of witches: those with innate supernatural powers, and others who developed them through training and learned traditions. Then, Hutton meets Magliocco's argument—of witches representing the evil in the universe and people's fear of it. The last characteristic of witchcraft, which was not only found in Europe but also in other cultures, was the possibility of resisting it.

Hutton states people can defeat witchcraft in three main ways: using benevolent protection magic, forcing the witch to retract from his or her spells, or destroying the witch by physical attack.

Hutton also highlights the importance of studying witchcraft in Western cultural traditions. On one hand, he affirms Europe is the only place where people both believed in witchcraft and officially stopped believing in it. Hutton affirms that Europe and the worldview, influenced by the Christian faith over the globe through the sequential colonisation waves in the 15th to 17th century to Asia and America, and then in the 19th century, spread to Africa and other parts of Asia and Oceania, consolidated a hegemonic conception about witchcraft and associating it to sorcery. Even though many cultural groups in the world believe and practice different types of mystical beliefs, it was only considered a crime and a sin in Europe (Hutton, 2017). Due to the Christian background, "practicing witchcraft is viewed as a crime against God and/or as a form of devil worship. Please note that, in some Christian communities, any non-Christian religion is also viewed as a form of devil-worship and/or a crime against God" (Aveytan et al., 2022). Therefore, for these same Christian communities, any non-Christian religious or mystical practice is perceived as a synonym for witchcraft.

The terms "witchcraft" and "witch" were considered historically to be of Eurocentric origin. This would imply an anthropological distinction between magic and medicine that is not suitable for every culture (Clifton, 2019). In this sense, Navajo culture, Ancient Egyptian practices, and shamanism, among others, are considered witchcraft from a Western Catholic-influenced bias. While for these cultures themselves, those same practices are their source of knowledge and healing.

Concepts of Witchcraft from the Old Testament

Witchcraft is a concept that has been around for millennia and it can be found in many ancient cultures and scripts. There are multiple references of witchcraft in the Old Testament—the first part of the Jewish, Catholic, and other Christian based religions bible. In the Old Testament of the Bible, there are several references to witchcraft and those who practised it. The Hebrew word for witchcraft is kashaph, which means to "practice magic". In the Old Testament, witchcraft is often associated with idolatry and a rebellion against God. Those who practise witchcraft are seen as having turned away from God and instead seek power and knowledge from other sources. The Bible also mentions the use of divination and necromancy, which are also referred to as forms of witchcraft. In summary, witchcraft is viewed as a sinful and evil practice in the Old Testament and those who engage in it, are condemned.

In Exodus 22:18, we see a reference to a woman who practises sorcery and divination, "Thou shalt not suffer a witch to live" (King James Version). This passage demonstrates the negative connotations associated with witchcraft and its practitioners.

In Deuteronomy 18:10–12, God warns against practising witchcraft or conversing with spirits, "[10] Let no one be found among you who sacrifices their son or daughter in the fire, who practices divination or sorcery, interprets omens, engages in witchcraft, [11] or casts spells, or who is a medium or spiritist or who consults the dead. [12] Anyone who does these things is detestable to the LORD; because of these same detestable practices, the LORD your God will drive out those nations before you." (New International Version). This passage requires no further translation, clearly showing how these practices are seen as a serious offence to God.

In the book of Exodus, Egyptian magicians were able to perform acts like Moses' miracles, and in the book of Daniel, Samuel, and Ezekiel, there is mention of dark or satanic powers. It recognises that human beings could establish a connection with those powers, which were prohibited and condemned:

> The Bible, too, recognises the possibility of human beings in their free agency making pacts with the devil, in virtue of which he was allowed, under divine administration, to share with them some of his supernatural powers as prince of the power of darkness, and God of this world. God condemned such pacts as unholy. Those who made them were called witches and wizards. (Kibor, 2006, p. 156)

According to Kibor (2006), the Old Testament refers to witchcraft by speaking about the pagan practices of Canaanites: those who did not belong to Israel, the people of God. Any belief in other supernatural forces of power, but the only true God, was then considered heresy, and therefore a sin.

The Witch of Endor is one of the oldest and possibly the most famous of all documented witches in history. The story is again mentioned in the Bible:

In the first book of Samuel 28:3–25, we see King Saul attempting to use witchcraft to gain insight into an upcoming battle against the Philistines. He asks the Witch of Endor to conjure up the spirit of the prophet Samuel. After much coercion from Saul, the witch agrees to perform the ritual, using a necromantic device known as an *Ekronite* or *pithom* that allows the soul of Samuel to be called forth from the underworld known as Sheol. Saul hears and learns from the spirit of Samuel that he will die in the battle and not gain victory. Astonished by what Saul is seeing and hearing, Saul immediately leaves, demonstrating his fear of the power of witchcraft.

Figure 2: Artwork depicting Saul, the ethereal presence of Samuel, and the Witch of Endor, created by William Blake. Public domain, via Wikimedia Commons (https://commons.wikimedia.org/wiki/File:The_Witch_of_Endor_(William_Blake)_2.jpg)

This scene has led many people throughout history to believe that this Witch of Endor had real magical powers and could actually raise the dead, cementing her in history as one of the earliest witches to be mentioned in a religious context. There is a view held that the Witch of Endor may also have had knowledge of astrology, divination, necromancy, and other forms of magic.

These previous passages demonstrate both positive and negative connotations associated with witchcraft, as well as the power of its practitioners. However, in general, it is clear that engaging in activities related to witchcraft was seen as a serious offence to God and was met with fear and apprehension.

This conception prevailed during the Middle Ages when the Catholic Church consolidated its power. The social and economic conditions of the major part of the population, including the lack of resources to ensure survival and a constant threat of death, resulted in an increase in pagan or folkloric practices. In the early modern period—15th and 16th centuries—the fear of witchcraft began to increase, mostly as a sign of social conflict. From the Christian perspective, witchcraft was associated with the Devil and devil worship. It was then that witch hunts, trials, and execution for witchcraft began. These views began to decline during the age of Enlightenment in the 17th and 18th centuries when social structures changed and new intellectual movements provided other explanations for the mysteries of life.

Magic and Magick

Magical beliefs have been a part of social life since the ancient ages. In early modern Europe however, the concerns about magic increased. While many people simply associated these practices with controlling nature or predicting the future, others, influenced by Christianism, associated magical practices with evil and demonic activity. Heinrich Cornelius Agrippa published *On Occult Philosophy* in 1531 and explained the concept of magic:

> Magic is a faculty of wonderful virtue, full of the most important mysteries, and containing the most profound contemplation of hidden secrets along with a knowledge of all of Nature—including its essence, power, quality, substance, and virtue. Magic instructs us on how things differ and agree with each other in order to produce wondrous effects by uniting the virtues of things through the application of them one to the other, as well as to lesser things affected by them, and joining and knitting them together by the powers and virtues of the higher beings (Lynn, 2018, para.11)

Magick is spelled similarly and has a related meaning, but it is not the same. From the paganism approach, magick has as a general meaning—all the "ritualisation of one's spiritual intentions" (The Pluralism Project of Harvard University, n.d.). According to this source, the letter "k" was introduced in the 20th century to distinguish magical practices from the fictional use of it. The site defines magick as:

> Cultivating supernatural powers, but rather about aligning oneself with natural forces to manifest an intention. In Paganism, ritual techniques that change a person's consciousness so that he or she may better perceive and participate in divine reality are regarded as magick (The Pluralism Project of Harvard University, n.d., para. 1).

The term Magick was also used by Aleister Crowley at the end of the 19th century. He founded a belief based on occultism. The word magick was used by Crowley to distinguish between traditional magic and his new congregation's practices. While for many scholars that have treated this issue, there is no significant difference, Crowley's concern was that magic was often related to illusionism and tricks that would lead people to believe that supernatural powers were responsible. For him, magick was "anything that moves a person close to fulfilling their ultimate destiny, which he called one's True Will" which does not need to be any metaphysical action or intention but anything that serves that purpose (Beyer, 2019).

Magick can take many forms, and can involve the use of symbols, words, gestures, and other tools to focus the practitioner's intent and will to bring about change. Some forms of magick involve the invocation of spirits or deities, while others do not.

Chapter 2: Famous Witches

(and those accused of Witchcraft)

History is full of witches whose names have transcended for various reasons. The following people were considered witches by their societies, perhaps with no reasonable justification.

Some characters of notoriety are:

Anne Boleyn

During the reign of Henry VIII, Anne Boleyn was accused of practising witchcraft to win Henry's affections. The accusations came from her enemies who sought to discredit and incriminate her. One of the most prominent charges against Boleyn was that she had used sorcery and enchantment to bewitch the King. Although there is no evidence whatsoever to support these claims, they were believed by some people at the time.

It has been reported that upon being arrested, one witness declared under oath that Anne was seen chanting incantations. This testimony was quickly dismissed as hearsay, but many believed it to be true. Although belief in magic and sorcery predated Henry VIII's reign, these beliefs were further popularised by his courtiers who sought to gain favour with the King by spreading sensational stories about his mistresses. As a result, Anne's enemies used this fear of witchcraft to discredit and incriminate her. In the end, whatever happened during

Henry VIII's court, it is clear that the accusations of sorcery against Anne Boleyn were baseless and unfounded. Anne was ultimately executed for treason.

Alizon Device and the Witches of Pendle

Alizon Device was a young girl from Lancashire, England, who was accused of witchcraft in the Pendle witch trials of 1612. She was one of ten people convicted and executed for the crime. The exact details of Alizon's life and her alleged witchcraft practices are not well documented, but her story has become infamous as a result of the attention drawn to the Pendle witch trials. Despite the lack of solid evidence against her and the others accused, Alizon and the other "witches" of Pendle were found guilty and executed in a highly publicised trial that helped to fuel the hysteria surrounding witchcraft in 17th century England.

The Pendle witch trials remain one of the most famous witch trials in England and the story of Alizon Device and the other accused witches has been the subject of many books and plays, and continues to interest historians and enthusiasts of the occult.

Margaret and Philippa Flower

Margaret and Philippa Flower were two English witches who lived in the late 16th century. They were highly respected by many within their community, particularly among pagans. The sisters were knowledgeable in herbalism and healing, which earned them a great deal of respect from both locals and clergy alike. They were also purported to have been able to see into the future, as well as being able to cast spells for money or love.

The charges brought against Margaret and Philippa Flower ranged from sorcery and casting evil spells to consorting with demons. Despite this, they still managed to gain sympathy from those around them due to their kind nature and willingness to help others. At their trial in 1589, both sisters defended their innocence and were eventually acquitted of all charges. Despite being exonerated, the stigma of witchcraft followed them throughout their lives but they remained true to their beliefs and never renounced them.

Agnes Sampson

Agnes Sampson was a Scottish healer and midwife who lived in the town of North Berwick during the late 16th century. In 1589, she was accused of being a witch by other women in the same profession. This led to her becoming the first woman to be officially accused of being a witch by King James VI of Scotland. Agnes was arrested, along with several other women, and put on trial for "conspiring with the Devil" to cause harm to the king and his subjects.

During her trial, Agnes denied all accusations made against her and attempted to prove her innocence by appealing to Church officials. Despite these efforts, and after being cruelly tortured, Agnes confessed these crimes and was sentenced to death. This sentencing was carried out in 1591 and Agnes was burned at the stake in Edinburgh's West Bow area.

While some believe that Agnes was the victim of a superstitious and misunderstood era, her story is still remembered today as a reminder of the dangers of witch hunts and religious persecution. The story of Agnes Sampson also shines a light on the mistreatment of women during this period in history, and how women were often judged differently than men.

Figure 3: An illustration found within James VI's Daemonologie (1597) unveils a depiction of witches, in the presence of the king. The artwork hints at the possibility of torture, offering a glimpse into the themes explored in the influential text. James VI and I (1566-1625), Public domain, via Wikimedia Commons (https://commons.wikimedia.org/wiki/File:Daemonologie1.jpg)

Isobel Gowdie

Isobel Gowdie was a self-proclaimed witch that lived in Scotland in the 17th century. Like Agnes Sampson, she was one of the most well-known witches in Scotland. Her story is particularly striking since it was her own detailed confession about her practices that led to her death. Isobel said she was able to transform into animals and was "entertained" by the Queen of the Fairies. There are different hypotheses about her confession, including that she could have suffered from psychosis, or that she was intending to receive merciful treatment by admitting to these fanciful crimes.

Isobel Gowdie was formally accused of witchcraft in 1662. She also confessed to a series of supernatural acts and dealings with the Devil, including enchanting cattle and making a pact with the Devil in exchange for magical powers. Isobel was tortured to extract a confession and these were used as evidence against her during her trial in which she was ultimately found guilty and sentenced to death. Isobel Gowdie was executed by strangling and burning.

Throughout history, women have been disproportionately targeted by witch trials due to their perceived connection with the occult and spiritual realm. In Isobel Gowdie's case, her gender likely played a part in her persecution, as it was assumed that women had more intimate connections with the supernatural world than men did. Additionally, many of the things she confessed to—such as using magic to make cows sick—may have been seen as a form of revenge against her male-dominated society, furthering the suspicion and fear of her.

Unlike many other accused witches, Isobel made detailed and elaborate confessions, describing her involvement in various occult practices such as shape-shifting, spells, and rituals. Her confessions were used as evidence against her and other accused witches, and have been seen as a sign of the severity of the torture and pressure that was put on her. It is believed that Isobel's confessions were influenced by the contemporary beliefs of the time, and that she may have been adapting her statements to conform to the expectations of her interrogators.

Like Agnes Sampson, Isobel's case was not based on any real evidence of witchcraft, but rather on superstitions, fear, and political or personal motives. At the time, the belief in witchcraft and the subsequent prosecution of those accused of it, was a way to control and terrorise the population.

Alice Kyteler

Alice Kyteler became a high-profile figure in 1324 when she became the first person to be accused of witchcraft in Ireland. Her accusers were her own family—sons that she had with her four husbands—which was suspicious activity enough for these times. The men had all died and the testimonies against her stated that she had used poison to kill them. Furthermore, she was accused of making sacrifices with animals to invoke Satan, and in using supernatural powers against Christians. The family asked that the bishop intervene on their behalf.

The bishop immediately began an investigation into Alice's activities and uncovered evidence that seemed to corroborate the accusations. It is recorded that he found several animals, including crows and cats, which had been killed or harmed by "mysterious forces". He also discovered remnants of what appeared to be ritualistic gatherings held in Kyteler's home. It was also learned Alice had been giving out, or selling, potions and charms, which supposedly granted people good fortune.

The evidence was enough for Alice to be arrested and to be brought before the bishop for trial. During the proceedings, there were many witnesses that declared against her, but Alice denied all charges of wrongdoing, witchcraft or sorcery. She proclaimed her innocence. However, due to the overwhelming evidence against her, she was eventually found guilty and fled the country, leaving her servant to face the punishment.

Marie Laveau

Marie Laveau is one of the most famous figures in New Orleans' history. Born in 1794, she was a Voodoo practitioner and Queen of her own religion. She had a reputation for being able to cast spells and hexes, as well as heal people through spiritual rituals. Her followers sought her services when they needed help with personal matters such as love problems or illness. Marie held religious ceremonies at her home every Sunday, drawing crowds from all over the city who believed in her power to cure them or solve their problems. People still flock to St Louis Cemetery No 1 today, where she is buried, hoping that visiting her grave will bring good luck. Many still believe that if you ask for Marie Laveau's help in the form of a wish, she will grant it.

Malin Matsdotter

Malin Matsdotter was a Swedish woman who was accused of witchcraft and executed in 1676. She is one of many people who were tried and convicted for witchcraft in Sweden during the 17th century when the country was experiencing a wave of witch hunts. The exact details of Malin Matsdotter's life and her alleged practices are not well documented, but her story is a testament to the fear and hysteria surrounding witchcraft during this time period.

Malin Matsdotter was known for her use of herbs and her knowledge of natural remedies. She is also credited with having prophetic powers, which she used to heal people suffering from illnesses and ailments. Malin's life and works were documented in the book "Witches of Värmland" by author Christine Christensen, which recounts her remarkable wisdom and skill. Some say that she brought hope to many people who had nowhere else to turn in their times of need. Despite being labelled as a witch at the time, Malin Matsdotter is remembered today as a wise healer who used her knowledge of herbs to help people.

Nostradamus

Nostradamus, born Michel de Nostredame, was a French astrologer, physician, and reputed seer who lived in the 16th century. He is known for his famous book "Les Propheties", a collection of cryptic prophecies that many believe predicted major historical events.

In the late 1530s, the Inquisition started to take notice of Nostradamus and his practises. The Inquisition was a powerful institution within the Catholic Church that was responsible for investigating and suppressing heresy. The Church was deeply suspicious of anything related to magic or the occult, and Nostradamus was no exception.

It was questioned whether all of Nostradamus's methods were based on pure medicine and science or if there was indeed witchcraft involved. Nostradamus was known to use a variety of unconventional methods, such as making astrological calculations using a type of scrying or divination called hydromancy, and creating medicines from various herbs and plants.

For those unfamiliar with the term, hydromancy is a form of divination that involves the observation of water, such as a lake, river, or bowl of water, in order to gain insight into the future or to receive spiritual guidance. The practise dates back to ancient times, and its use has been recorded in many different cultures and traditions. The practitioner will typically gaze into the water and look for patterns or images that may reveal information about the future or answer specific questions. This may involve interpreting the movement of the water, the reflections of light, or shapes and colours that appear on the surface of the water.

In 1554, the Inquisition summoned Nostradamus to appear before them to answer questions about his methods and beliefs. Nostradamus was able to satisfy the Inquisition that his work was based solely on natural methods and that he was not involved in any kind of witchcraft or occult practises.

Although Nostradamus was able to clear himself of any charges, the incident reflects the deep suspicion and fear that many people had about the occult and magic during the 16th century. Nostradamus continued to practice medicine and astrology until his death in 1566, and his prophecies continue to fascinate and intrigue people to this day.

Mother Shipton

Mother Shipton's real name was Ursula Southeil and she lived in England in the 16th century. As she had a crippled figure, people believed and said that she was the Devil's daughter. Besides her disturbing appearance, she was a prophetess and predicted events like the shipwreck of the "Spanish Armada, the Great Plague of London, the Great Fire of London, the execution of Mary Queen of Scots, and the Internet" (Polkes et al., 2019). This last prophecy is taken from her words: "'around the world thoughts shall fly in the twinkling of an eye'" (5 Real Witches in History, 2014).

Mother Shipton became famous during her lifetime for these prophecies and predictions, which were widely circulated throughout England in pamphlets and broadsides. Despite controversy surrounding some of her predictions and their accuracy, she gained fame and notoriety through the 16th century and into the present day as one of Britain's most well-known witches.

In addition to predicting great events such as wars and plagues, Mother Shipton was also known for her skill in herbalism and healing. She was said to have concocted potions and remedies to treat a variety of ailments. Some believed that she used these remedies to bring on death or illness when an enemy thought to cross her path. Mother Shipton passed away at the age of 73. Because the Church did not allow her to be buried in consecrated ground her grave has been lost to history.

La Voisin (Catherine Monvoisin)

Her real name was Catherine Monvoisin, and she lived in France in the 17th century. She was one of the most notorious figures in the French witch trials, accused of practising black magic and satanic rituals. Monvoisin was a physician who practiced midwifery and also accused of performing abortions. It is not surprising that her knowledge of medicine and these practices would make her look like a witch. She also had knowledge of substances and was famous for her poisons. Monvoisin was a member of a secret cult—*affaire des poisons*—whose members had poisoned members of the French aristocracy and who even tried to kill King Louis XIV.

Her trial resulted in her conviction and eventual execution by burning at the stake. While no evidence of actual sorcery was found during her trial, it was speculated that she had performed rituals to "influence events", engaged in the trade of love spells and charms, performed divination, and taken part in rituals focused on revenge.

Chapter 3: Witchcraft Practices

Both witchcraft and sorcery have been around since ancient times. There are however, important differences between them. After a review of the different conceptions of witchcraft, it should be pointed out that as a general meaning, witchcraft refers to various practices that involve invoking supernatural forces or spirits to obtain a particular result—either for the good or the bad. Sorcery, as one variant of witchcraft, is more closely related to using occult powers to harm others.

The Differences Between Witchcraft and Sorcery: The Good and the Evil

In modern times, witchcraft is often seen as a form of a nature-based spiritual practice that involves the use of herbs, symbols, rituals, and spells for healing and protection. It focuses on using the energy of nature to achieve a desired result or outcome. Sorcery, on the other hand, is viewed as being more focused on the manipulation of supernatural forces for personal gain. This type of magic leans more towards malicious intent and can involve curses, hexes, dark rituals, and other forms of malevolent spell casting. Therefore, witchcraft is typically seen as being a positive practice—it is associated with connecting with natural energies to create balance and harmony by aligning with the will of nature. Sorcery, on the other hand, is seen as being a dark art because it involves using supernatural forces for selfish purposes and disregards any ethical considerations.

There are anthropological distinctions between the two concepts. The cultural and social background of both terms and practices need to be considered. While "witchcraft exists as a form of scapegoating and accusations—a method of explaining causation and healing, or avoiding, social rifts", sorcery refers to "a pragmatic, conscious practice, involving acts of magic and leading to personal power for the practitioner" (Moro, 2019).

Regardless of the differences between witchcraft and sorcery, it is important to remember that both are powerful traditions with a long history of use.

We have already discussed the concept of a witch in mediaeval Europe. In the folkloric version, for the peasant population, the term defined women who were believed to have magical healing powers. However, this version also described them with the ability to fly and transform into animals. These ideas and the relationship between witches and the Devil were fed by the testimonies and confessions that woman accused of witchcraft rendered, either due to people's imagination, or to the effects of torture over the prisoners' wills. For many scholars, common ideas about witches can be explained through the analysis of social structures, as they were characters that reflected social conflict (Moro, 2019). Regardless of the particularities found in different cultures, the "lists of characteristics associated with witches anywhere in the-world might include nocturnal activity, flight, community meetings or sabbats, and ritual murder" (Moro, 2019).

The following chapters will cover the reasons why it was women that were mostly accused of witchcraft. However, people that performed witchcraft during these times were also men. They are called wizards or warlocks, though the words are not synonyms. Wizards have a positive connotation. The term is rooted in the Middle English word *wysard*, which means "wise". Therefore, wizards are wise men that provide good advice to people and use their knowledge about natural forces and magical powers for virtuous purposes (Czarina 2022). On the other hand, "warlock" is based on the Old English word *waerloga,* meaning "oath breaker" (Czarina, 2022). Unlike wizards, warlocks use dark powers to deceive people, or to serve selfish and immoral objectives. In medieval times, the term was used to describe men who were thought to have made a pact with the Devil. Warlocks were often depicted as being malicious and using their powers to harm others.

The main difference between wizards and warlocks is the perception of their intentions and motivations. While wizards are often seen as benevolent and helpful, warlocks are typically associated with evil and malevolent intentions, much like the sorcerer. In modern times, the word warlock has been reclaimed by some practitioners of witchcraft and Wicca to simply describe a male practitioner of magic. However, many still associate the term with the negative connotations of the past.

The same opposition between the evil and the good use of magical powers also applies to women. Beyond the distinction, due to the moral nature of the power and the objectives, women magicians are distinguished by their own attributes and how they achieve them. While witches have—or might have—innate conditions, sorceresses "typically must learn the texts, practices, rituals, or other components of magic as understood in their culture; such knowledge is esoteric and not normally available to everyone" (Moro, 2019). However, the main characteristic of sorcerers and sorceresses is that they use magic to cause harm.

Classifying Witchcraft Practices

Witchcraft practices can be classified according to the intention or type of pursued goals, the powers they invoke or are involved in, and the type of resources and techniques displayed by the witchcraft practitioner. As stated before, some of these practices have the intention to protect, explain or twist human fate, or influence the will of a person, but also witchcraft can have the explicit purpose of hurting others.

Witchcraft and sorcery can also invoke diverse sources of power. Some practices rely upon benevolent spirits, while others are supported by a dark or occult influence or power. Some practices require physical contact or the use of diverse elements and substances to manipulate metaphysical energy, while others can be displayed only by the power of the mind, words, or any other contactless intervention.

Practices that involve any sort of magic have some common characteristics:

- A particular practitioner acts as an agent of spiritual or supernatural energy.

- A certain use of language and actions that breaks with conventional rules and creates a mystic atmosphere.

- Singular use of a special language and speech register which is not accessible or decipherable by common people.

- The knowledge and use of herbs, substances, and different types of materials (talismans, runes, and crystals, among others).

- "Altered states of consciousness induced by chanting, fasting, or herbal draught" (Waterman, 2017).

Witchcraft practices come in a variety of shapes and forms, from traditional folk magic to neo-paganism. While the tools used vary from culture to culture, some of the most common methods are divination, spell casting, using charms or talismans, and communing with spirits. Divination is the practice of seeking knowledge through supernatural means such as tarot cards, runes or Ouija boards. Spell casting involves harnessing an inner power to create certain effects in the world around the caster. This may include chanting, burning herbs or candles, or other rituals designed to bring about desired outcomes. Charms and talismans are also used as it is believed they contain magical properties that help protect their wearers from harm or bad luck.

Communing with spirits is the practice of engaging in communication with entities from other planes or realms. This is achieved through rituals such as seances and trance work. All of these practices have been used for centuries and have played a major role in many religious traditions around the world.

Different cultures interpret and practise witchcraft differently, but there are several core beliefs that are shared among many practitioners:

- That everything has an energy which can be tapped into for healing, knowledge and protection.
- That the universe is ever-changing yet interconnected and that manipulating energies contained within the surrounding universe can bring about desired results.
- That communication with other realms is possible through rituals like meditation, chanting, or trance work often with the help of magical herbs.
- That certain symbols and objects have a special power that should be respected.

While some may view witchcraft as an evil pursuit, it is important to remember that those who practise it are often seeking to improve their lives and the lives of those around them. With respect and open-mindedness, one can learn a great deal about this fascinating craft by exploring its rich cultural history.

Spells and Charms

Spells are one of the most common witchcraft practices, and consist of a set of words written or pronounced. They are believed to invoke metaphysical powers that are capable of provoking certain effects. According to several sources dated in the Middle Ages in Europe, spells are often invocations to the Devil or other sorts of demons or dark entities. Spells are believed to have an effect, simply because it is a witch or wizard, sorcerer or sorceress that pronounces them. They are often passed down through generations with instructions on what to say, and how to say them.

Spells are often lyrical compositions, with connotative meanings that can only meet their true and complete meaning when they are pronounced or delivered in a specific way. According to mediaevalist scholarly studies, spells are a combination of ritual and poetry that intend to alter people's consciousness to predispose them to believe that a magical event can occur. Spells have a typical structure to achieve that effect. According to Waterman (2017),

> They use performative language in Old English verse, magical numbers (multiples of 3), and a characteristic rhythm combining the alliterative structure of Old English verse with counter rhythms that index its special status as magical. There is a lot of repetition (para. 9).

There are spells to dominate nature, attach lovers, increase fertility, protect from evil or injuries, and even prevent other spells' effects. In the early Modern Age, spells and charms were considered evidence of the malefic powers of those who pronounced them.

Charms are objects or words that are believed to have magical powers. They are used to protect, heal, or bring good luck to the user. In ancient times, charms were often made from natural materials such as stones, bones, and herbs, and were believed to have the power to ward off evil spirits and protect against disease. For example, in ancient Egypt, the scarab beetle was considered a powerful charm because it was believed to represent rebirth and renewal. During the Middle Ages, witchcraft was often associated with magic charms and they were used to ward off witches, demons, and other supernatural beings. These charms were often made from metals, such as silver or gold, and inscribed with magical symbols and incantations.

In the 16th and 17th centuries, the use of magical items was heavily persecuted in Europe and America. Many people who owned such items were accused of witchcraft. In modern times, the use of magical charms continues to be popular among many practitioners of witchcraft, particularly in Wicca and other neo-pagan traditions.

Rituals and Rites

According to the dictionary, rituals are "the established form for a ceremony" (Merriam-Webster, n.d.). In general, the concept applies to any religious or mythical ceremony of a procedure that is repeated and sacralised as a requisite to achieve a certain goal. They can imply words, gestures, objects, and some need to be performed by qualified people—in the case of witchcraft, by those who have the power to invoke supernatural energies—some rituals need to be performed in special places or on certain dates to have an effect.

Many rituals have been established and developed within communities throughout time. There is another associated term—rite. For many cultures, rites are a sequence of rituals with different social meanings that imply at some level, a connection with the inanimate world (Walker & Berryman, 2018). They are characterised by formalism, invariability, and performance that become crystallised by repetition. Rituals can adopt variants according to different cultural frames with similar meanings. Some current thinking considers these rituals as creative processes that accompany natural change. As Bado-Fralick (n.d.) would put it, "Witches are quite consciously focused on the transformative nature of ritual processes and aware of their own creative efforts in bringing about the desired transformation". There exists the belief that there is a slight line that separates witchcraft rituals from other expressions of human beliefs in metaphysical powers (Bailey, 2006).

Anthropological studies retrieve artefacts and materials used in rituals and argue about the relationship between witchcraft effects and people's beliefs.

The materials used in rituals can be projectile points, crystals, shells, and others, depending on the cultures. These are considered ritual technologies. Walker and Berryman (2018), explain that:

> When put into ritual action, contribute to performance characteristics of releasing, attracting, and repelling spiritual forces including witches. Projectile points and pigments offer protection against the most powerful of witches. The colours of projectile points and shell facilitate the sympathetic link between the power of spirits of the directions (places) and these materials (para. 104).

There is no rational way to prove the connection between witchcraft rituals and their effectiveness, but they are a constitutive part of their practices.

Levitation and Flying

One of the most common and widespread images of witches is flying, often with the aid of magical artefacts such as a broom. The picture of witches with the ability to fly was fed by the folkloric conception of witches. It grew among the peasant population in Europe as a way to distinguish witches that invoked evil powers, from those who helped people to release pain and illnesses. Regardless of this connotation, it continued to grow during the Modern Age and with the prosecution of people accused of witchcraft.

Levitation is a paranormal effect that implies that a body of a person or of an object can rise from the ground and remain floating in the air by mystical means or at least, irrational means. The ability to levitate is not limited to witchcraft, but it is also claimed as an attribution of specially chosen people in different religions over the globe belonging to varied cultures.

Flying on brooms, sticks or other magical artefacts has been linked to practitioners of folk magic and witchcraft since at least the Middle Ages. Witches were believed to use these objects to fly off and attend meetings with their fellow sorcerers in faraway lands. In some cases, the witch was thought to be able to achieve flight with no help from an outside source—using only her own magical powers. The ability to fly was sometimes seen as a sign of being chosen by supernatural forces or as proof that a particular witch was particularly powerful.

In modern times and popular culture, witches are often depicted flying—usually as part of a humorous or light-hearted scene. While the idea of witches being able to take flight may seem far-fetched and fantastical, it is important to remember that many cultures around the world have long embraced this concept as part of their spiritual belief systems. Thus, for many people, the idea of witches taking flight is one that is rooted in centuries of folklore and tradition. It is an image that continues to captivate and fascinate us today.

The link between witchcraft and flying has also been explored in literature throughout the years—from classic works like Shakespeare's Macbeth to more recent fantasy stories such as the Harry Potter series. In these stories, we are shown how powerful magic can be when used for creative and imaginative purposes.

Magic

From an anthropological perspective, magic is seen as a primary stage of human society's progress. According to Moro (2019),

> Magic was a precursor to religion and science. Given that it assumes primitive people used magic as a way of explaining causality, their approach is often labelled as intellectualist. Magic was a way to explain things that could not otherwise be understood or accounted for (Moro, 2019, para. 7).

People's need for understanding and controlling the world around them led to the development of magical thinking to fulfil these necessities.

Bailey (2006) agrees with this statement, considering that magic refers to a whole system of ideas that "provides a means for navigating among the varied forces that comprise and shape material creation, and promises its practitioners methods of controlling or at least affecting those forces". Each society decides and establishes the limits for what shall be considered validated explanations of the world and beliefs. They also decide what will fall into the realm of superstition, unreal, or mere fantasy. In the same way, societies have determined the magical thinking that is allowed, and which is illegitimate, censored, and sometimes condemned.

Magic can be distinguished from other mystical beliefs and practices, as they mostly consist of private and secret acts instead of being public and involving the community (Bailey, 2006). Then, people expect immediate effects from magical practices as a confirmation of that in which they believe. In a nutshell, magic can be considered the general concept that encompasses any belief and practice that implies a connection or invocation of supernatural powers. With their particular nuances, witchcraft and sorcery are included in the magic realm despite not being limited to them (Bailey, 2006).

Runes and Sigils

Both runes and sigils are elements that compose a system, a language that allows interpreting the present and predicting the future. They are used to create a channel of communication between the material world and the metaphysical dimension: "Sigils and runes have been bridging the gap between everyday communication and the mind-body-spirit realms as far back as humanity's story can be traced" (Marr, 2022).

The origins of Runes can be traced to Germanic and Nordic tribes from Northern Europe—Scandinavia and Britain—and the oldest evidence dates from the 2nd to the 8th centuries. The word means "mystery, whisper or secret and it's a form of divination or oracle reading system that's used to help gain insight into situations or questions" (Newcombe, n.d.). Those tribes used runes for magical purposes.

Runes can be printed or written on many different types of material including stones, jewellery, and weapons, among others. Even though they are a system of symbols, the runes represent letters of an alphabet. However, they are not considered a writing system. They do however, combine to create messages. There are several studies that intend to find equivalences between runes, symbols, and the Latin alphabet to translate or transliterate old scriptures from ancient Germanic and Scandinavian cultures (Knirk & Williams, 2010). Many cultures have used runes to cast spells and to make prophecies, since people believed spirits use the runes to communicate with human beings.

Although they are also a means of communication, sigils are of a different nature and are used differently from runes. A sigil is "a symbol that has magical power—where the intent is the driving force that carries the message of the sigil into a manifested reality" (Marr 2022). They can be used to invoke benevolent or dark powers, depending on the intention of their creator. Its use consists of "a step-by-step process of setting intention, creating a sigil, charging the image, releasing it, and forgetting" (Marr 2022).

Magical Herbs

Plants have been a natural resource for human beings from ancient times. The understanding of the cycles of nature and the properties of plants was essential for survival. They were, from the beginning, not only a source of food but also to treat illness. According to Martinelli (2020),

> Since our earliest origins, people have used plants for all kinds of purposes, including food, medicine, fibre, art, housing, and ritual. Our spiritual connection to plants has led humans to incorporate them into ritual and prayer, weaving the energies of plants into the creation of our cultural identities (para. 1).

The knowledge about the properties and uses of plants and herbs gave a halo of wisdom to those who possessed them, and natural properties were perceived as magical. Many plants have a supernatural history either because they have the power to protect or to cause harm (Shade 2022). Robinson Herb Garden at Cornell University has a collection of herbs that have been used for supernatural purposes.

Artemisia

In witchcraft, Artemisia has many magical uses such as "luring love, cleansing, protection from accidents and evil spirits, and divination" (Ellis, 2021). It also has hallucinogenic effects.

Artemisia, also known as mugwort, has long been used in folk medicines and rituals by cultures all around the world. In ancient times, it was believed to have healing powers and protect against evil spirits. Today, modern science has found that Artemisia contains compounds with many beneficial properties. The active compounds in Artemisia are terpenes, flavonoids, and sesquiterpenes. These compounds help the herb fight infection, reduce inflammation and act as an antioxidant. Studies have shown that Artemisia may even be effective in treating certain types of cancer and other diseases caused by oxidative stress. It can also be used as an antifungal, antibacterial, and antiviral agent.

Deadly Nightshade

Deadly Nightshade, or Belladonna as it is commonly known, is an herbaceous perennial plant believed to have been used in witchcraft since ancient times. It is a deadly poisonous plant. However, it is still used today medically. It has a component capable of regulating the heart rhythm and can also be used to dilate the pupils. The plant has a hallucinogenic effect and historically people prepared an unguent used in witchcraft, since it provoked the feeling of flying.

Deadly Nightshade has long been associated with powerful forces, such as curses and hexes, and the power of nature. The leaves of Deadly Nightshade were also thought to be able to turn people into animals, while its roots were—correctly—believed to bring on sleep and death.

Figure 4: An illustration of Atropa Belladonna, commonly known as Deadly Nightshade, is featured in Köhler's Medicinal Plants (1884). Public domain, via Wikimedia Commons (https://commons.wikimedia.org/wiki/File:Atropa_belladonna_-_K%C3%B6hler%E2%80%93s_Medizinal-Pflanzen-018.jpg)

Henbane

Henbane, scientifically known as Hyoscyamus niger, is a flowering plant that is native to Europe. It has been used medicinally for centuries, but is fatally toxic if consumed in excess. In traditional medicine, henbane was used to treat conditions such as pain relief and anxiety.

Henbane has a long history of use in witchcraft, dating back to ancient times. Henbane was also used as a flying unguent in witchcraft. It is a dangerous plant due to its effect on the nervous and respiratory systems. It was believed to be a powerful tool for casting spells, divination, and protection from evil spirits. The plant itself was used in many forms as an ingredient in medicinal potions, as incense burnt during rituals, and ingested by witches as part of their practices.

Henbane was thought to have the power to transform its users into other shapes or animals when mixed with certain ingredients. This belief is likely rooted because henbane contains toxic alkaloids which can cause hallucinations or delirium if consumed in large doses. Despite all the potentially dangerous side-effects, henbane remained popular among witching circles due to these perceived magical properties.

Poppy

For centuries, witches have been drawn to poppies for their powerful magical properties. Many cultures associate poppies with death and rebirth, which makes them useful in rituals related to banishing negative energies or casting off old habits. They have also been used for protection spells, or to invoke luck or financial success. Poppies are also a popular ingredient in love spells, as the petals are thought to draw in positive energy and aid in reconciliation. The poppy flower also has protective powers according to Ancient Greek mythology.

The narcotic properties of the poppy were also used for medicinal purposes—mainly for treating pain and insomnia. Poppies have also been used for divination. In some traditions, their seeds are scattered on the ground and interpreted according to their patterns or shapes. Ground up poppy seed pods can also be mixed with water, then strained through a cloth into a bowl. It is said that images of future events will appear on the surface of the liquid.

Vervain

Vervain, used by several Mediterranean cultures, had the primary role "to protect believers against evil spells or negative energy and to purify sacred places, such as altars, ceremonial implements, temples, and private dwellings" (Shade, 2022).

One common use of magical herbs like vervain is by burning during rituals, allowing the smoke to spread throughout a room to provide protection from negative energies. Many believe plants like vervain contain natural elements that can help ward off unwanted visitors like ghosts or spirits. Vervain, and other types of incense, are often used to fill the air with the aromas given to create a peaceful atmosphere. This is also known as smudging—a purifying and cleansing ceremony.

Mandrake

Mandrake is a plant that has been associated with witchcraft and the occult for centuries. It has a long history of use in traditional medicine and folk magic, and is considered to be a powerful herb in many cultures.

The mandrake root is often found shaped like a human figure. This has led to many legends and superstitions surrounding the plant. In European folklore, it was believed that the mandrake root had the power to bring good luck, protect against evil spirits, and aid in love and fertility. It was also believed that the root could be used to make a potion that would reveal the truth or make someone fall in love.

Charms, Amulets and Talismans

Amulets and talismans are words often used as synonyms although they have some differences. In general, they are natural or handmade objects "believed to be endowed with special powers to protect or bring good fortune. Amulets are carried on the person or kept in the place that is the desired sphere of influence" (Encyclopaedia Britannica, 2022). While amulets have innate powers, talismans need to be charged with protective energy and they need a qualified person—a witch or wizard, for instance—to intervene in their preparation. There are other differences that can be highlighted about these protective artefacts: "Talismans are exclusively defensive, and are manufactured to create a protective aura around the person bearing it. Amulets have the function of absorbing negative energy directed at their bearer. Both work as catalysers for good and bad vibes" (Gaspar, 2013). Their nuances vary from one culture to another.

According to Magliocco (2018), there are certain patterns among amulets and talismans. Her studies focused on amulets that protect from the evil eye, but she bases her conclusions on further studies of other cultural features. Her studies suggest that horns and "Phallic symbols such as fish, roosters, daggers, snakes, and keys are also commonly found on protective amulets" (Magliocco, 2018). Some suggest that this is due to the relationship established between protection and masculine power or strength.

There are many amulets, most of them originally destined to prevent the harm that the evil eye could cause.

- The Mano Fica, used since the Ancient Roman Empire, represents a gesture of a thumb caught between two fingers. Its meaning is also linked to the phallic symbol and masculine power.

- The Mano Cornuta, also used in Western Europe in the Ancient Age but also in other cultures, resembles the exalted horns of an animal. In some cultures, such as in Italy, it is believed to ward off evil or bad luck, and it is sometimes accompanied by the words "corna" or "corno", which means "horn".

- The Hamsa, or Hand of God, is an amulet used by Christians, Jews, and Muslims. It means "five" in Arabic, and it is represented as a hand with five fingers extended and an eye in the palm. It protects not only against evil, but also appeals to good fortune, fertility, and abundance.

- The Mano Pantea—or pantheistic hand—is a set of amulets crimped in one. Its base is again a hand with the signal of the sacerdotal benediction, which is also believed to provide protection. This signal is given by the thumb, the index and middle fingers extended. Then, the hand is covered with several amulets that can vary. The most common are birds, frogs, snakes, a knife, and human figures.

During the witch trials of the 16th and 17th centuries, people accused of witchcraft were often searched for amulets and talismans, which were considered evidence of witchcraft. Many were forced to give up their amulets and talismans or were punished.

In contemporary witchcraft, amulets and talismans are still used for protection. They are often made from natural materials, such as stones, crystals, or wood, and are inscribed with symbols or words that are believed to have magical properties. For example, the pentagram is often used as a symbol of protection and is a five-pointed star with a single star pointing upwards. A pentacle and a pentagram are two different things, and they are often confused. When a pentagram is enclosed in a circle, it is known as a pentacle.

Figure 5: The formation of a pentacle emerges as a pentagram enclosed within a circle, forming the symbol sometimes referred to as "the endless knot". Public Domain via Wikimedia Commons (https://commons.wikimedia.org/wiki/File:Pentagram_(endless_knot).png)

In neo-pagan religions and Wicca, the pentacle is a representation of the five elements—the earth, the air, fire, water, and spirit. The design represents the concept of balance and harmony, and the five points of the star represent the balance between the elements, or directions. You will note that the cover of this book features a pentacle.

Potions

Considering its etymology, *potion* can mean "medicine" from the Old French term *pocion*, or "drinking", according to its Latin origin in the term *potionem*. However, the meaning also has a

Spanish version that links it with the term *Panza,* which means "poison" (Harper, n.d.).

A potion is a liquid that has particular properties that can either heal or harm depending on the components. The knowledge about herbs and substances, and how to mix them to obtain certain results, gives those who have it extraordinary powers. For many cultures, people who had the knowledge and ability to produce potions with supernatural—or unexplainable powers—were considered witches or wizards. For some, it was a motive for respect and admiration. For others, a reason for fear and revulsion.

In different societies throughout time, the production and administration of potions was illegal. The most common administrators of potions were quacks, pharmacists, or apothecaries, and those considered witches or wizards. There is a thin line between potions with real effects and supposedly magical preparations. Quacks were considered to deliver and sell fake elixirs that deceived people, while the others based their liquids on their knowledge of herbal properties. There is also a cultural component that includes people's beliefs in particular social conditions. Crises and epidemics led people to believe and trust these magical preparations, since there were no better scientific solutions and healthcare was not available for all the social levels.

There are different types of potions depending on the expected result. There are love potions, to attract or make a lover come back, or to make a relationship last. There are also healing potions, destined to treat illnesses and pains. Two of the most famous are the Confectio Alchermes and the St. Paul's potion. The first one was delivered to treat madness and depression, and the other was used to cure epilepsy. Mount (2015) states.

> Although this sounds like a real witch's brew, most of the ingredients do have some medicinal value: liquorice is good for the chest—it was and continues to be used to treat coughs and bronchitis; sage is thought to improve blood flow to the brain and help one's memory, and willow contains salicylic acid, a component of aspirin (para. 2).

There were potions to cure all types of afflictions such as sore throat, stomach ache, migraines, and cough among others. Hallucinogenic potions were based on the natural properties of some herbs and plants and were used in rituals and witchcraft practices. According to Müller's investigation (1998), several herbs from the family of the Solanaceae (Nightshade family) were used for medical purposes, but also in all sorts of rituals and magical uses. While these plants have an anaesthetic effect, in greater doses, they induce delirium and also death.

Scrying and Divination

Witchcraft is related, in some part, to the human need to control the future, avoid misfortune, and anticipate what might come. Therefore, scrying or divination has always been one of the main practices of witchcraft. Divination is not always related to witchcraft. Nostradamus and Joseph Smith (the spiritual leader of the Mormons) are believed to have had the ability to read the future or interpret divine meanings (Smith, 2016).

Divination and scrying are mostly used as exchangeable terms, though there are some slight differences.

Divination "is a magical procedure or ritual designed to find out what is not knowable by ordinary means; such as the foretelling of the future by interpreting omens" (Avetyan et al., 2022). In comparison, scrying is a type of divination that involves a medium that perceives images from the future by staring into a reflective surface such as a speculum, mirrors, crystal balls, or even water (Wigington, 2019). Note that in this meaning, a speculum is whatever surface is chosen as the scrying method.

There are many types of divination that are performed by using different methods and instruments that can project images from the unknown future. Some of these types include cards—like Tarot or runes; bibliomancy—which uses books to answer questions, tea leaf reading, astrology, or interpreting animal behaviours (Avetyan et al., 2022). Using these instruments is accompanied by a ritual and it requires specific techniques.

However, divination and scrying are not only about predicting the future but also about the search for answers and explanations for present and past conditions, and revealing secrets (Smith, 2016).

Figure 6: The Magician, an illustration sourced from the Rider-Waite tarot deck's initial release in 1910. The artwork portrays a figure of a magician, surrounded by symbolic elements that evoke the mysteries and powers associated with the tarot. Pamela Colman Smith, Public domain, via Wikimedia Commons (https://commons.wikimedia.org/wiki/File:RWS_Tarot_01_Magician .jpg)

People from all times and cultures have been fascinated by mirrors. Some used to believe that the reflected image was a demoniac version of the person, and many spells and formulas repeated in front of a mirror would invoke malign entities (O'Gieblyn, 2019). Some others consider mirrors a way to connect with forces from other levels of energy. In a passage from Sedgwick (2020),

In the medieval era, people were considered too 'unclean' to speak to highly evolved beings like angels. They needed a device that blurred the barriers between the spiritual and physical realms. Mirrors were just one of those devices (p. 45).

According to several anthropological studies of different societies, some would perceive the image reflected in the mirror as the soul, while others consider it an alternative self with the ability to transcend the material world (O'Gieblyn, 2019). Besides this association of mirrors with eternity or immortality, these objects are also used for divination and predicting the future, in particular black mirrors. They are less reflective than common mirrors, and that is why many clairvoyants use them. For example, there is a dark mirror in the Museum of Witchcraft in Cornwall, England, which belonged to the founder of the museum, Cecil Williamson. Though there is no evidence of how old the mirror is, it might be from the 1820s (King, 2017).

Whichever scrying method is used, it is believed to work by allowing the user to enter a state of trance or altered consciousness, which enables them to receive psychic impressions or messages from the spirit realm. The images and symbols that appear are thought to be symbolic representations of the unconscious mind of the user or of the forces and energies at work in the world.

Although scrying is often associated with divination and fortune-telling, it can also be used for self-exploration and personal growth, as well as for creative inspiration and artistic expression. Some people also use scrying as a form of meditation or spiritual practice to gain insight into their own spiritual path.

Necromancy

The practice of necromancy is documented in numerous ancient writings and cultures:

- Its origins can be found in Sumerian religion and mythology—the texts present Anu, the god of death, who was regarded as having the ability to bring the dead back to life.

- The extensive use of mummification and the complex burial rites intended to honour the deceased are indications that the ancient Egyptians also engaged in necromantic practices.

- The Odyssey by Homer contains the first mention of necromancy in Greece. In the eleventh book of The Odyssey, the main character and hero of the poem, Odysseus, travels to Hades, the underworld. He performs a ritual and makes sacrifices to the dead in order to consult the blind seer Tiresias for advice. Odysseus learns from Tiresias that his journey back to Ithaca will be filled with difficulty.

- The cult of Hecate—a goddess connected to death and the underworld. Adherents were known to engage in ritualistic summoning of spirits and communication with the dead.

According to the Merriam-Webster (n.d.) dictionary, necromancy is directly related to witchcraft and sorcery. It is a "conjuration of the spirits of the dead for purposes of magically revealing the future or influencing the course of events." Encyclopaedia Britannica (2022) describes it as a practice that can be traced back to ancient cultures such as the Babylonians, Egyptians, Greeks, Romans, and Etruscans (ancient people of Etruria, Italy), and was later popular in Western Europe in the late Middle Ages and during the Renaissance period.

Under this source, necromancy was a practice performed by magicians who looked for desolated places to use a consecrated circle. Being inside the circle, they were able to pull away from them the "anger of the spirits of death" (Britannica Encyclopaedia, 2022). Also, they carried out certain practices with dead bodies of victims of violent deaths: "the corpse was thought to retain some measure of unused vitality, and so the use of parts of corpses as ingredients of charms came to be an important technique of witchcraft" (Britannica Encyclopaedia, 2022). All these practices were condemned by the Catholic Church. A study about the importance of necromancy in Medieval Europe reveals necromancers performed several magical practices that included divination, rituals that led to hallucination, rites to release pain, sacrifices, and sympathetic rituals among others (Giralt, 2017).

Many people with knowledge of anatomy and physiology, most of whom came from the Orient into Europe, were considered necromancers, and for that, they were persecuted and rejected. This was the early stage of modern medicine, and these necromancers were the first physicians. They experimented with and studied dead bodies to learn about the organs and the function of the human body. For the Catholic Church, death was nothing but God's will and they rejected this practice—considering it a sin and punishable by excommunication, or even death. Its practitioners were accused of witchcraft and heresy.

The practice of Necromancy continues today in some forms, usually through various occult practices such as conjuring spirits or holding seances in order to seek guidance from those who have passed on. It is worth noting that although some may view Necromancy as dark or even nefarious, many cultures have used it to commune with the dead—either out of curiosity or reverence—since time immemorial.

Familiars

A familiar is an object or an animal that represents small demons that were given to witches by the Devil (Witgington, 2018). For other sources of witchcraft literacy, familiars are magical helpers that assist magicians or witches in supernatural ways to accomplish their tasks and claim shelter and food for compensation (Stavynska, 2021). In a more general sense, any person can have a familiar: an animal with which the person can connect with its particular animal spirit (Witgington, 2018). According to Parish (2019),

> Familiars were evidence of the permeable boundary that existed between humans and animals, the presence of demonic ritual and blood-feeding among practitioners of magic, the moral and theological depravity of witchcraft, and the transgression of nature that lay at the heart of the witch (p. 135).

However, they were a more common component of the popular imagination about witches in England, and of less relevance in continental Europe.

A common belief among witches is that they can communicate with their familiar through telepathy—a kind of mental conversation between two living beings. In witchcraft tradition, the animals that most usually serve as familiars to witches are cats—black ones in particular. This conception of cats as the preferred animal to become a familiar was fed by many traditions that consider black cats to be emissaries of bad fortune.

Other animals can also be inhabited by supernatural powers such as dogs, toads, or other small species. Cats were especially related to witchcraft in the Middle Ages in Europe because many of the women who were accused of witchcraft happened to have one as a pet. Cats were very common then, and they had already been blamed for adversity. During the Black Death, people believed cats were responsible for spreading the disease and thousands of cats were killed (Why are cats associated with witches, 2015). This was a great mistake since the real cause of the illness spread was the overpopulation of rats, or more specifically, the fleas that they carried. In fact, cats would have helped to constrain the infection by killing the very things that were causing the disease in the first place. However, there was no way for people to know that at the time.

Familiars were often thought to be supernatural creatures, capable of communicating with their witch owner and providing them with additional magical powers. In some cultures, familiars could shape-shift into animals. Familiars could also act as messengers between the witch and the Devil, bringing back news from Hell or performing malicious deeds at their master's bidding. The familiar was seen as an extension of the witch's power and spirit—acting as a guardian, advisor and assistant in times of need. Witches believed their familiars protected them from evil spirits while helping them perform magical rituals and spells. Some even used their familiars to cast curses on their enemies or to seek knowledge from beyond the grave. They were considered an important part of a witch's life and power.

The Witches Grimoire

A grimoire is a book of spells, conjurations, and instructions to perform magical rituals. In ancient times, these books were used by herbalists and alchemists to practice their craft. Instructions on how to use magical items like herbs would be recorded. The oldest known grimoire is the Greek Magical Papyri, which dates back to the 2nd century BC.

Throughout history, various cultures have produced their own versions of grimoires, each with their own unique flavour of magic and lore. In Europe during the Middle Ages and Renaissance periods, grimoires were popularly used for divination such as scrying and recording predicted future events. They were also used in the practice of astrology and to document remedies for health issues. Due to the secretive nature of these ancient texts, they remain shrouded in mystery. Many believe that these books are powerful gateways into the supernatural world and reveal secrets that would otherwise be impossible to uncover.

Some use the term grimoire to refer to the Book of Shadows, as used by those who practice Wicca, but the meaning is wider than that (Brethauer, n.d.). According to Owen Davies, professor of Social History at the University of Hertfordshire, the origin of the word is based on the French word *grammaire,* which is used to refer to books written in Latin. In 18th century France, many books that circulated were written in French. This, in addition to the popular tradition of believing in magic and witchcraft, made the term *grammaire* change and turn into *grimoire* with a different meaning: As outlined by Brethauer (n.d.),

> It was used as a figure of speech to denote something that was difficult to read or impossible to understand, such as, "it is like a grimoire to me". It was only in the nineteenth

century, with the educated resurgence of the interest in the occult, that it began to enter general English usage (para. 8).

There are grimoires from all times including Ancient Egypt, Greece, and Rome. Many grimoires that date from the Middle Ages were nothing but manuscripts that belonged to people who experimented with magical practices "and were often created by figures called Ceremonial magicians. Ceremonial magicians, like the famous John Dee, were not enemies of the Christian church like you might think. Many were wealthy individuals who experimented with the intersections between science, faith, and magic" (Johnson, 2021, para. 9). Therefore, while any book that contains spells and magic content can be considered a grimoire, it can be affirmed that a grimoire is historical in nature (Johnson, 2021).

In more modern times, grimoires have evolved into books of instructions for activities such as magical rituals and spell work. Such grimoires often provide instructions on how to summon spirits and communicate with them. Grimoires also have been known to contain information about various spiritual concepts, like reincarnation and karma. Grimoires have been adapted for use with modern practices such as Wicca and neo-paganism. These practices often incorporate many of the same concepts and instructions found in traditional grimoires but with a more contemporary twist. The modern-day witch might find guidance on how to cast spells or perform rituals, while a practitioner of

Wicca might discover information on deities and symbols associated with their faith.

The Witches' Sabbath

The Witches' Sabbath has a long and complex history dating back to the Middle Ages. A witches' sabbath is a gathering of witches whose purpose is to perform rituals. In Western Europe, the belief in witches gained special importance between the 14th and 15th centuries, and the conception of witchcraft became more and more sinister. Then, the idea of the sabbath referred to a ritual where (Schoonmaker, 2015),

> Witches were summoned to attend a ceremony where Satan himself and other demons would be present in human or animal form. Each witch was required to profess their undying loyalty and service to the Devil and make a full renunciation and rejection of the Christian faith in return for being taught the 'black arts' (para. 2).

The term Sabbath itself comes from Jewish tradition, referring to the weekly day of rest and worship. Unrelated to this, in medieval Europe, witches were thought to gather on their Sabbath night, often during a full moon or a new moon. On these nights, they would engage in dark rituals that could bring them into communion with the Devil. These gatherings were believed to be held in remote locations such as forests or caves. The activities at these events ranged from dancing around fires, singing magical chants, casting spells, and conjuring spirits. It was also said that witches could even shape-shift into animals during their Sabbaths.

According to Hutton's (2014) research, the image of the witches' sabbath keeps a tight relation with the influence of the witch trials that took place in Europe and how they impacted people's imagination.

Hutton (2014) proposes that the idea of the witches' sabbath has its origins in mediaeval Europe and it refers to nocturnal processions or cavalcades of spirits. This was later named "Wild Hunt" by Jacob Grimm. The darker connotation of the sabbath is due to the leverage of folkloric ideas on the Wild Hunt, which is "the cavalcade of dead souls believed to roam the countryside at night in search of animal and human prey" (Wilby, 2013). The historical context plays a central role in the construction of the meanings in the collective worldview.

At that time, the witches' sabbath is related to dark practices. It implied the encounter of the witches' bodies and souls with the Devil, other rituals with human remains to practise transmutations, and other procedures to induce death, requesting the Devil's appearance in all possible ways, renouncing Christ, performing ritual eating, drinking, and dancing; and the breaking of sexual conventions.

Despite the folkloric and imaginary components that the witches' sabbath encompasses, Schoonmaker (2015) considers that in some contexts, it had a real social and political dimension: "While some view this spectacle as an attempt of authorities to rationalise heretical matters they could not comprehend, in the age of witchcraft there was a very genuine and widespread understanding of magical practice and the Sabbath."

Figure 7: "Preparation for the Witches Sabbath". Painted by David Teniers the Younger, portrays a scene where a witch engages in potion-making under the watchful gaze of her familiar spirit. Various spell-casting objects rest upon the floor, while another witch reads from a grimoire, simultaneously anointing another witch who is about to take flight on an inverted broom. Public domain, via Wikimedia Commons (https://commons.wikimedia.org/wiki/File:Hexenszene_1700.JPG)

It is thought that the practice of the Witches' Sabbath became less common once Christianity became more widespread throughout Europe. However, over time, the notion of a sinister gathering of witches grew more elaborate. In popular folklore, writers began to include mythical creatures such as demons and fairies at these events and evil and malevolent activities such as human sacrifice or drinking blood.

The *Maleficium*, an Act of Sorcery

The *Maleficium*, or Act of Sorcery, is an ancient concept that has been present in many cultures throughout history. In ancient times, people believed the maleficium was the use of supernatural powers to cause harm or misfortune to others. In many cultures, this practice was associated with witchcraft and was often seen as a form of black magic.

The word Maleficium originated from the Latin *malefic*, meaning "evil doing" or "magical harm" and today it is still practised in some parts of the world. In Europe during the Middle Ages, it was considered to be especially popular among those who were thought of as "wise" or "enlightened". Those accused of sorcery were harshly punished, leading to the belief that it was a dangerous practice.

The Maleficium is a magical practice linked to sorcery that has a harmful and destructive connotation. Then, it is malevolent magic that, for Western cultures, involves the Devil or any other evil powers. In the early Modern Age, the practice of maleficium was defined to justify and condemn people—mostly women—accused of witchcraft and it emphasised the association of witches with the Devil (Hillis, n.d.).

In some societies, the maleficium or bewitchment is "an occult interaction between two people, and it is either accompanied by some actual deed or not" (Blécourt & Davies, 2020). It implies that people suffering from misfortune can blame other people's intention to harm them. Then, the damage is not the result of the maleficium but that which explains the unfortunate circumstance. In other cultural contexts, the maleficium covers the social function of administering justice and controlling social order. Here, the maleficium does not involve two persons, but someone with the power to provoke it, and the community (Blécourt & Davies, 2020). Besides these meanings, the *maleficium* can have several intentions besides the wish to cause harm such as recovering properties, influencing the will of other to obtain a benefit, or even obtaining good things as a result, for example, making someone recover from illness.

The practice of the Maleficium has evolved over time as different cultures adopted their own unique forms of sorcery. In some countries, elements from certain religions are incorporated into the spells and rituals associated with this magical art form. The Maleficium is both fascinating and controversial; while some view it as a form of spiritual growth, others see it as a dangerous activity that should be avoided at all costs.

The power of the Maleficium continues to intrigue people today and many still seek its secrets, hoping to unlock its mysteries and gaining greater control over their environment.

Chapter 4: The Origin and Evolution of Witchcraft

The origin and evolution of witchcraft is complex and has been the subject of much debate among scholars and historians. While the exact origins of witchcraft are not known, it is believed to have emerged in prehistoric times as a form of animism or nature worship. As human societies became more complex and organised, witchcraft evolved into a more formalised set of beliefs and practices, often associated with shamanism and the use of magic. Despite efforts to suppress it, witchcraft continued to evolve and adapt. This was particularly true in rural areas where it was often intertwined with nature, the seasons, traditional folk beliefs and practices passed down through generations.

It is important to highlight that, for some scholars, witchcraft is a concept used to name different phenomena according to the culture or society it is practised within. Given this, witchcraft in Medieval and early Modern Europe, the practices of African tribes, present Wiccan, paganism or indeed any other practice or belief system, should not be treated as the same, or reduced to a single pattern. Instead, they should be studied and analysed separately (Moro, 2019).

Throughout this and the following chapters, we shall attempt to cover the singularities of different phenomena related to witchcraft whilst considering its cultural and historical background.

Witchcraft in the Middle Ages

In Europe, witchcraft came to be associated with the Devil and evil spirits during the Middle Ages, leading to a period of intense persecution and witch-hunting that lasted for several centuries. Many innocent people, mostly women, were accused of witchcraft and executed.

As presented in Chapter 1, magical thinking has always been a resource for human beings to deal with the unexpected and as an attempt to control fate. From an evolutionary perspective, magical thinking is a stage of human knowledge that searches for answers for those things that are beyond human reason—before religious thinking. This implies a complex and organised system of coherent ideas. Later, societies would replace these explanations that accounted for supernatural forces with rational arguments and empirical evidence. Every society in human history has had, and still has, a concept of witchcraft (Mesaki, 1995).

From a Eurocentric Christian perspective, witchcraft had a negative connotation that again was formed during the Middle Ages. The influence of Christianity, at this time, attributed the term and the practices with a dangerous and evil nature. However, for other cultures, even now, the meaning of witchcraft is more connected to a spiritual level. For many societies, witchcraft is considered as a set of "religious traditions that connect them to the spiritual world and give people a sense of hope and faith" (Avetyan et al., 2022). As discussed in the previous chapter, in Europe, the word witchcraft referred to a crime of *maleficium*: a performance that used supernatural powers to harm others (Mesaki, 1995). It is the "culmination of centuries of linkage drawn by Christian authorities between the performance of magic and demonic forces," explaining the difference between magic—witchcraft with this negative connotation—and religious beliefs (Bailey, 2006).

As Magliocco (2018) points out, many witchcraft practices were, for many peasant people, the only access to healthcare. In the Middle Ages, medicine hadn't evolved yet, and the knowledge and treatment for diseases were unattainable for most of the people. A reliance and help from local wise women who knew the healing properties of herbs, who prepared potions, and were able to ease pain, was required. They were called *cunning folk* and played an important role in mediaeval societies. There are cultural reasons that led to associating cunning folk with witchcraft. For example, according to *Witchcraft, Women & the Healing Arts in the Early Modern Period: Wise-Women & Cunning Folk Healers* (2022), "Many of these such healers were illiterate, and so they came up with rhymes and songs to remember their concoctions, which may have inspired the witches' spells found in literature and myth".

Later, in the 18th and 19th centuries, medicine and modern science evolved, but their discoveries and cures for diseases were still out of financial reach for the majority of the population. Therefore, they continued to turn to the cunning folk. They received from them remedies, amulets, and charms to protect or heal illnesses (Savage, 2017). Besides these cunning folk, others would also tell fortunes, or sell spells to achieve all kinds of goals.

There are many popular practices and traditions that are confused with magic or witchcraft. They have a common thread. All of them are delivered from a magico-religious approach and perspective. They all resort to irrational or supernatural forces to explain phenomena and, sometimes, attempt to gain control over the material world. However, there is a significant difference between folk magic and witchcraft. Folk magic, like any folk practice, is performed by people—anyone can do it—and the wisdom is inherited from the cultural legacy, passed down through generations (Folk magic and witchcraft | What's the difference, 2016). These folk practices include songs, prayers, festivals, and celebrations, among others. Also, folk magic does not have spiritual or religious connotations. It does not require the work of a "creator". While witchcraft is considered a set of beliefs, folk magic syncretises cultural ideas. Moreover, folk magic does not involve complex or elaborate rituals, instead, it is more based on daily stuff and common sense (Folk magic and witchcraft | What's the difference, 2016).

Shamanism

Historians and anthropologists have used the term *shamanism* to describe a set of beliefs and practices that involve individuals, known as shamans. These practitioners interact with supernatural forces in order to address spiritual, psychological, or physical ailments. Shamans perform these functions within their community for the betterment of the people. Over time, the term was adopted by anthropologists to describe similar practices found in other cultures around the world.

There is no single definition of shamanism that encompasses all of its variations. Many scholars do however agree that it involves practices such as journeying, chanting, ritualistic dancing, and the use of psychoactive substances. These practices are required in order to enter altered states of consciousness and interact with spiritual entities. Shamanism is found in many cultures and regions, including among the indigenous peoples of North and South America, Siberia, Africa, and Oceania.

European scholars found the term useful for studying these indigenous cultures and to make a distinction from other European practices. However, shamanism is a polysemic term. Its origins can be traced back to the period between the 13th and 16th centuries when travellers reached the region of Siberia where the term originated (Hutton, 2006). Shamans receive different names depending on the culture: "seers, medicine men, witch doctors, or occasionally witches" (Shamanism, Witchcraft, and Magic: Foreword, 2006). What makes them all fall into the category of shamanism is "the ritualised activities, trance states, preternatural abilities, and supposed interaction with spiritual entities (demons, ghosts, etc.)" (Shamanism, Witchcraft, and Magic: Foreword, 2006).

Studying the American Apache people, Singh (2020) found some relevant differences between shamans and witches. While both had extraordinary features, witches displayed their practices in private. Instead, shamans are people with public power and perform a public demonstration of this. For the Apache people, witches were evil, and they feared them. However, they respected the shamans since they predicted when the community was in danger, they cured illnesses, and provided advice and guidance. Singh (2020) considers that both shamanism and witchcraft represent the particularities of these types of practices as determined by the cultural and historical context. Retrieving Boyer's contribution, Singh (2020) highlights "shamanism and witchcraft beliefs as 'wild traditions' or 'informal religious activity'—magico-religious traditions that are widespread, that likely predated modern doctrinal religions, and that reappear when powerful organisations try to quash them."

According to several scholars (Magliocco, 2009; Avetyan et al., 2022; Bailey, 2006), witchcraft's origins derive from a legacy of ancient people's beliefs and ancestral traditions. Collectively, these first transformed into folk practices. Later, into other religious practices—creating a new role for wise women and cunning folk to play in the community.

Stregheria

Stregheria is a popular pagan religious movement that draws its inspiration from the pre-Christian folk traditions and the beliefs originating from Italy. The term stregheria comes from the Italian word *strega*, which means "witch". Stregheria is not a single organised religion, but rather a loosely defined set of beliefs and practices that vary widely from practitioner to practitioner. Some parts of stregheria draw heavily from historical Italian witchcraft traditions. Other parts incorporate elements of Wicca, ceremonial magic, or other pagan traditions.

One of the central beliefs of stregheria is the veneration of ancestors and the spirits of the natural world, including animals, plants, and the elements. Stregheri (the practitioners) also practice divination, spellwork, and herbalism, and may work with a variety of deities and spirits, both Italian and non-Italian.

Stregheria has gained some popular attention in recent years through the works of authors such as Raven Grimassi and Leo Martello. It has, however, also been the subject of controversy and debate within the wider pagan community. Whatever the disagreements are, those who practice stregheria assert that it provides a deeply meaningful and personal spiritual path that connects them with their ancestral roots, the natural world and their beliefs.

Some scholars recognise in stregheria the origins of witchcraft before the predominance of the Catholic Church. Grimassi's hypothesis is that stregheria is a continuation of pre-Christian popular practices in Italy. The goddesses Diana and Dianus are their principal deities, and Aradia as their prophet (Magliocco, 2009). Magglioco points out that stregheria is now a popular spiritual movement of Italian immigrants in America who have symbolised rituals inherited from their familiar traditions.

Witchcraft and Satanism

Despite the many connotations of the term witchcraft, there are several practices that fall within the concept. The association between them and malevolent supernatural forces became stronger in Europe in the early Modern Age. At that time, any practice that invoked spiritual forces outside Christianity was considered heresy and satanism. The accusation of witchcraft became a crime within the legal system, and the formal characterisation of witches' stereotypes synthesised popular images of them flying, interacting with familiars, and making pacts with the Devil. As stated by Parish (2019), "In the hands of demonologists, inquisitors and law-makers, the multiple components of the archetypal witch crystallised around the imagery of the 'demonic pact', the personal relationship between the witch and devil, and the all-encompassing vocabulary of *maleficium* which made real these ideas in popular culture and social communities" (p. 84).

However, the links between witchcraft and satanism, or even the invocation of evil forces and demons, are not essential components of its nature. Beliefs and practices aimed at Satan belong to a different current. According to Sluhovsky (2018), in the European context, the idea of Satan was used to explain or justify evil, and to dissipate political or economic crises. Satan—or the Devil—is, according to Christian and Judaism traditions, the embodiment of evil, the antithesis of God and Christ (*Britannica Encyclopaedia, 2022*).

Satan, as the embodiment of evil, had previously appeared in the Zoroastrian religion, in the figure of Angra Mainyu or Ahriman, the opposite of their god, Zoroaster (Satanism, History.com).

In Jewish pre-Christian beliefs (Satanism, History.com),

> The name 'Satan' first appeared in the Book of Numbers in the Bible, used as a term describing defiance. The character of Satan is featured in the Book of Job as an accusing angel. In the apocryphal Book of Enoch, written in the first century B.C., Satan is a member of the Watchers, a group of fallen angels (para. 5).

Before the 17th century, it was difficult to determine the singularity of Satanist practices since the limit is blurred by the Christian accusation of satanism to any other religious belief or magical folk practices. Sluhovsky (2018) commenting on Introvigne's book (*Satanism: A Social History*), points out that satanism is a modern phenomenon whose origins can be placed at the end of the 18th century when the French Revolution was claimed to be Satan's work. Following his theory, in the 19th century, followers of Satan, anti-satanic fanatics and satanism hysteria, and artists with an interest in satanic issues, proliferated in Europe and it is difficult to recognise real spiritual currents (*Sluhovsky, 2018*). In the 19th century, satanism also rekindled the idea of Satan as an anti-hero and was used by critical political currents (Satanism, History.com).

Modern Satanist beliefs do not take Satan as the reincarnation of evil. Instead, they base their beliefs on an idea of anti-Christian ideals and values, which hark back to a pre-Christian way of life. They claim to be atheistic, agnostic, or deistic and do not necessarily advocate or exercise evil, although they allege "extreme forms of individualism and ethical egoism and may reject traditional Abrahamic religions, particularly Christianity, as hypocritical and repressive" (Britannica Encyclopaedia, 2022).

In the 1960s, Anton Szandor LaVey led a counterculture group and founded the Church of Satan in the United States. He became popular, appearing on television, sharing his ideas, and attracting the attention of thousands of people, including celebrities that joined his religious organisation. LaVey did not preach evil or relate Satan with the Christian conception of him as the embodiment of evil. Instead, he talked about the "Infernal Majesty" which was a symbol of rebellion against social injustice and authority. Its bases are laid on atheism and agnosticism and expressed against the conformism of other religions that charge individuals with guilt and remorse (Kaelber, n.d.). LaVey motivated his followers to increase a self-centred attitude and strengthen their egos to leave aside their weaknesses and submission (Melton, 2022). LaVey compiled his religious ideas and rituals in The Satanic Bible in 1969.

Figure 8: The Sigil of Baphomet, the emblem of the Church of Satan. At the centre of the sigil is the image of a pentagram, a five-pointed star, enclosed within a circle. The pentagram points upward, with two points extended upward, representing the horns of a goat. Provided by GTRus - Public Domain via Wikimedia Commons (https://commons.wikimedia.org/wiki/File:Baphosimb.svg)

In the 1980s and 1990s, there was a noticeable backlash against the Church of Satan in the United States and the United Kingdom—called the 'Satanic Panic'. There were wrong assumptions and beliefs about their practices, and Satanists were accused of over ten thousand crimes (Kaelber, n.d.). This accelerated after the publication of a book entitled 'Michelle Remembers'. After this, testimonies about these sorts of crimes where Satanists were alleged to have played a role proliferated. However, there was no evidence brought forward that proved that there was an organised net of satanic cults to perpetrate these crimes (Shewan, 2017). The possible influence and consequences of Satanists' practices on people's mental health are still a matter of controversy. Others say that this is a flimsy accusation and allege that satanism does not promote or practice evil.

Luciferianism

There is another religious current associated with Satanism, with some differences—mainly seen in their system of beliefs and historical roots. Luciferianism is a belief system that centres around the figure of Lucifer from the Abrahamic religions, who is often seen as a symbol of enlightenment, knowledge, and rebellion against oppressive authority. Also described as "an entity representing various interpretations of 'the morning star' as understood by ancient cultures such as the Greeks and Egyptians" (Ford et al., n.d.). As Christianity began to spread throughout the continent during Mediaeval times, some people continued to practise these ancient traditions, but now under the guise of Christian symbolism and theological teachings. This gave rise to what we now know as modern Luciferianism.

There are some figures or beliefs that may be seen as analogous to Luciferianism in certain ways. For example, some people see Prometheus from Greek mythology as a similar figure to Lucifer. He, too, defied the gods and brought knowledge to humanity. Similarities can also be drawn with Lilith in the Jewish Talmud, who began as a female demon but is seen as representing human aspirations and freedom confronting god's powers. Others may draw parallels between Luciferianism and the figure of Satan in Christianity, as both are often seen as rebellious and associated with knowledge and free will.

It is important to note, however, that these analogies are not perfect. The specific beliefs and practices of Luciferianism differ significantly from those of other belief systems, even ones that on the surface, like Satanism, appear analogous. It is also important to approach these comparisons with respect and an open mind, and to recognise that different people interpret these figures and belief systems in different ways. Regardless of the many differences between witchcraft, Satanism and Luciferianism, not only about their beliefs and practices but also their historical development, there is still a trend toward presenting them as in the same current. While there are some similarities between Luciferianism and other belief systems or figures, each belief system is unique and should be understood on its own terms.

Luciferianism's principles are based on Gnosticism and its proposition of a reversion of the good and evil relationship for human beings. "The formula for this inversion is reflected by the narrative paradigm of the Gnostic Hypostasis myth. As opposed to the original Biblical version, the Gnostic account represents a revaluation of the Hebraic story of the first man's temptation, the desire of mere men to 'be as gods' by partaking of the tree of the 'knowledge of good and evil'" (Collins, 2006). As a result, for Gnosticism, human beings do not wish to be like gods. Instead, they reinforce men's powers and their capability to develop science through reason.

As stated, Luciferians believe in personal transformation through the pursuit of knowledge, which is seen as the ultimate source of enlightenment. They place a strong emphasis on enlightenment through self-discovery and exploration, rather than relying on established religious doctrines or teachings from authorities. Luciferianism also emphasises the importance of creative expression, individuality, and exploring new ideas and experiences. The Luciferians have their own set of rituals, festivals, and ceremonies that bring about personal growth and understanding. These include honouring the four elements—earth, air, fire, and water—as part of their spiritual practice. The Luciferian belief system also places great value on the power of astrology, ritual magic, and other forms of divination to help individuals gain insight into their lives and understand universal truths.

One of the most remarkable references of Luciferianism is from Madeline Montalban, an English astrologer, tarot, and esoteric practitioner. In 1956, she and her husband, Nicholas Heron, founded the Order of the Morning Star (OMS), a magical system that based its principles upon Luciferianism. They preached worship to Lucifer or Lumiel, considering him a benevolent angel, and other angels related to the planets of the Solar System. She was a prolific writer and many of her works were published in editorials of minor circulation. Her organisation became influential among London occultist groups but later decreased after her death in 1982. The organisation was to be revitalised in the later decades by different scholars and writers interested in occultism.

The Luciferian movement has seen a resurgence in recent decades, as more and more people seek alternative spiritual paths that offer freedom from the constraints of traditional religious beliefs. While its adherents are still few in number compared to other religions, the Luciferian faith is slowly gaining ground as more people embrace its teachings and philosophies.

Luciferianism remains misunderstood by those outside of the faith, with many incorrectly associating it with dark forces or evil. In reality, Luciferians view Lucifer as a symbol of knowledge and personal liberation rather than an embodiment of darkness and wickedness.

Wicca

Wicca is a modern form of witchcraft which incorporates components from both ancient and contemporary spiritual traditions. Wicca places a strong emphasis on a love of the natural world and a commitment to self-empowerment. It has however, attracted much public interest as a result of its connection to witchcraft. There are some key elements of Wicca:

- Wicca was developed in England during the first half of the 20th century.

- The practitioners of Wicca are called Wiccans and they share with Luciferians the belief that magic has the power to change the world for the better.

- Wiccans worship both a goddess and a god but also recognise the divine presence in all facets of existence, including nature, humanity, and the cosmos—it is a nature-centred faith.

- Wiccans celebrate the cycles of nature and the seasons, and perform rituals and ceremonies to mark important events and transitions.

- Wiccans adhere to a code of ethics known as the Wiccan Rede (a very loose code of actions), which emphasises the importance of living in harmony with nature and doing no harm to others.

- Wicca has a diverse community with many different traditions and practices, and it continues to evolve and grow in the modern world.

There is a massive presence of witchcraft in pop culture through social media and other cultural products that may or may not be truly related to witchcraft and Wiccan practices. Witchcraft has become fashionable, and the limits between witchcraft, Wicca, and other practices seem to blur. Wicca and witchcraft fall within modern pagan movements (Berger, 2021). However, Wicca is not strictly the same as witchcraft, as explained previously. According to Pearson (2000), Wicca is a different practice from witchcraft and has no relation with the early modern phenomena in Europe during the witch hunts. Furthermore, it is not an awakening of old paganism that is displaced and obliged to hide with the consolidation of Christianism either.

For some scholars, it is controversial to categorise Wicca as a religion (Kealber, n.d.). Some consider Wicca as a specific form of spiritual expression linked to an esoteric religious tradition that began to grow in the 17th century, contrasting the rationality and denial of magic of the European Renaissance (Pearson, 2000). It is stated that Wicca represents the triumph of magic over rationality and the resistance of spirituality in a world dominated by materialism and scepticism. Indeed, Wicca is considered by some as the face of the New Age Movement, together with witchcraft and neo-paganism. Pearson (2000) points out that practitioners of Wicca consider it an esoteric mystery religion, but distinguish between themselves and the practitioners of exoteric witchcraft and paganism. Also of note is the further scholarly research carried out by Kealber (n.d.), who affirms the view that many practitioners of Wicca consider that it does draw upon pagan practices and that it is indeed the renewal of an old religion. As stated at the beginning of this book, controversies will remain.

It was Gerald Gardner who created a branch of Wicca in 1954 and asserted that it was "the continuation of ancient Celtic, Druidic and Pagan practices, that had to go underground to survive the Christian persecutions in the 1700s" (Kealber, n.d.). More will be discussed of Gerald Gardner and Wicca in chapter 12. While one academic current considers that it was a singular movement to resist the advance of rationality, the other affirms they were practitioners of an ancient pagan religion hiding from Christian persecution. However, both currents situate their origin in the 18th century.

During the 20th century and in the early 21st century, magic and pagan practices had become more and more popular, Wicca among them. Pearson (2000) points out that in the 20th century, Wicca merged with other forms of paganism and witchcraft, and that by 1996, 10,000 people were considered Wiccans in Britain. According to Berger's (2021) research, at the time, there were approximately 800,000 people in the United States that consider themselves Wiccans, and these numbers keep growing. While before the 1970s, Wicca was linked to paganism, from then on, they continued through different paths as two separate organisations.

Regardless of Wicca's categorisation as a religion or not, it is a deist set of beliefs. It has two central deity figures, a male and a female—a god and a goddess—representing a balance within nature. However, these deity figures do not have a singular representation; instead, they can take the shape of gods from other religions. The female is a three-form goddess—the Triple Goddess—representing the different aspects of women's attributes: innocence, compassionate love, and wisdom. The man is the 'Horned God', retrieving several ancient devotions of virility and masculine strength.

Wiccans have their own version of the afterlife, similar to Buddhist reincarnation. With this belief, people come back after death endlessly as a part of the cyclical nature of the universe.

Wicca has a deep connection with natural elements and their rituals include those involving the earth, the air, water, fire and spirit. All these components are incorporated in the Pentagram, the Wicca symbol. It uses a five-point star with one pointing up, which represents the triumph of the spirit over matter.

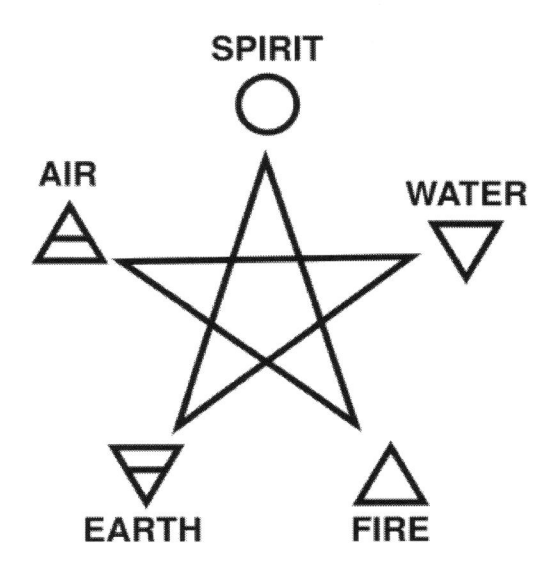

Figure 9: Pentagram showing the Five Elements. Provided by Jakub Jankiewicz - Public domain, via Wikimedia Commons (https://commons.wikimedia.org/wiki/File:Five_elements_and_pentagram.svg)

For Wiccans, magic is not a manifestation of supernatural powers; instead, it is the energy in nature that enables them to perform an extraordinary transformation of things. According to Kealber (n.d.), they also believe in something similar to *karma*. This is documented in the Wiccan Rede.

> Any magical spells one casts will come back to you threefold. For example, a helpful spell can give you great fortune, but a harmful spell could effectively be your own undoing. In fact, this concept applies to all actions, not just magical ones, and can mean either an effect you cause will return to you with three times its force, or that it will affect you in mind, body, and spirit (p. 4).

Unlike most religions, Wicca does not have a common moral basement and they are not required to gather within closed hierarchical or formal organisations. Wiccans are also free to behave as they wish with a general key statement, again from the Wiccan Rede, which states, "if it harms none, do what you will" (Kealber, n.d.). Where there is organisation, it is based on covens led by a priest or priestess, who will be a more experienced Wiccan. There is not a centralised figure of authority or roof organisation; instead, as Pearson (2000) explains, Wicca has not developed a fixed hierarchical structure; instead, it is organised in small groups and fluid networks. These groups, the covens, are the units of Wicca and reflect the flexibility for their members to experience and practise their beliefs as they want. Each of the covens performs its practices individually, although there are occasions that can be shared by a greater community.

Rituals often take place within purified magic circles marked on the ground and follow cycles of nature. Each coven group can perform these rituals according to their own beliefs and traditions. The most common and standardised of the Wiccan rituals is the Wheel of the Year. The Wheel of the Year represents the annual cycle of solar events and seasonal changes through the 365-day cycle. These events are celebrated by festivals such as Yule in December and Samhain in November.

Witchcraft, Feminism, and the Media

Witchcraft has been historically linked to femininity and is often used as a symbol of female power. Witchcraft is also related to resistance movements and in the latter decades, witchcraft gained a new significance regarding the empowerment of women. In this sense, the image of the witch—usually presented as a repulsive figure in the folk mediaeval imagination, is no longer a popular held view. This image of the "traditional character of a witch" is only present in conventional popular celebrations like Halloween or in movies and television programs. The image that embodied what society feared or wanted to eliminate, now becomes a symbol of powerful women.

For some scholars, it still has a connotation related to certain roles given to women in Western societies, placing them as villains. This observation applies to the popular cultural expression of how a witch should look, behave, and the role they play. It is worth noting that the majority of the villains in traditional fairy tales are played by women, either as witches, or bad stepmothers or sisters. These characters serve as foils to the heroic protagonists, and their motivations and actions provide insight into the cultural and societal values of the time in which the stories were written. Some notable examples include:

- The Evil Queen from Snow White. A jealous and vain queen. She seeks to kill Snow White, her stepdaughter, because she fears that the beauty of the young princess will surpass her own.

- The Wicked Stepmother from Cinderella who mistreats and abuses Cinderella. She prevents Cinderella from attending the ball and tries to keep her from marrying the prince.

- The Witch from Hansel and Gretel. This evil witch lures the two siblings into her house and plans to eat them.

- The Fairy Godmother from Sleeping Beauty. While not traditionally seen as a villain, the Fairy Godmother places a curse on the young princess that causes her to fall into a deep sleep on her 16th birthday.

There is a common pattern in Western patriarchal societies that have accused transgressive women of being witches. They were persecuted or even executed, probably as a public exemplary punishment, to discourage others from challenging the current social order. The figure of the witch has been used in several ways throughout time to deepen and reinforce gender inequalities to the detriment of women (Rosen, 2017). Media, and other means of the cultural industry, have played a central role. Disney movies, for instance, presented an iconic contemporary representation of witches and were a crystallisation of older social stereotypes that despised women who were unable to have children, giving women the unique social role of mothers (Rosen, 2017). Then, their physical representation was created from different social stereotyped patterns: "Physical attributions that correspond with age, socioeconomic status, or deviance were used as tools to incriminate women who fit into those categories" (Rosen, 2017).

In the 1990s, there seemed to be a new trend that presented a public image of witches as empowered women, and it was presumed that these characters had a feminist message. The television shows Charmed, Buffy the Vampire Slayer, and Sabrina the Teenage Witch are usually considered examples of the influence of the Third Wave of feminism on massive cultural products, presenting witches as empowered women. These works depicted witches who used their magical powers for good, creating strong independent characters that resonated with modern feminist ideals.

Though for some scholars, it only contributes to increasing confusion on the empowerment rhetoric (Trammell, 2020). These programs have an early precedent in the 1960s. The show, Bewitched, was the first one to be displayed on television with a new insight on witchcraft. It is usually placed in the Second Wave of the feminist movement (Harris, 2020). While these programs present a fresh image of witches as beautiful women with a place within communities—unlike traditional witches that were excluded—Bewitched still represented gender stereotypes that neglected women (Harris, 2020). The programs of the '90s presented a new convention: empowered women are young and beautiful (Trammell, 2020).

Recent feminist waves all over the globe vindicate the images of witches as a symbol of how patriarchal societies stigmatised and disregarded women. In their public representations, they used the slogan "we are the granddaughters of the witches they couldn't burn" as a way to symbolise that all women were considered witches within societies that marginalised, underestimated, and despised them (Toon, 2021). The intersections between popular culture and popular feminism are complex, and while its presence in media provides visibility and encourages social debate, it can also be feeding a marketing use of feminism, jeopardising the original goal of social change.

Feminist ideas about witches are not only present in mass media and pop culture but also have a strong influence on some branches of Neopagan communities. Spajić (2020) carried out research regarding feminism and Neo-paganism and she highlights that most known religions are male-dominated, in particular the Judeo-Christian tradition. This is clear not only in the God figure, prophets, and main characters but also in those who alone can socially interpret God's words, such as a priest or rabbi.

Following her interest in women's possibilities to express their spirituality, Spajić narrowed her study to Neopaganism as a new religious wave. Throughout her research, she found that

Neopaganism, being a decentralised organisation, was not affected—or at least, less affected—by gender roles division. These women were able to perform rituals and have a more active role than in other religions (Spajić, 2020). Spajić goes on to suggest that Neopaganism can be a movement to women's empowerment but works better as a place where empowered women can find a safe community and somewhere to experience spirituality.

Neo-paganism is an umbrella term that includes different polytheistic religions that reinterpret and revive pre-Christian traditions (Spajić, 2020). According to Magliocco (2014), these religions actively embrace magic "as a set of spiritual techniques to change consciousness at will, and they use it to re-enchant the universe, expand human potential, achieve self-realisation and planetary healing, and ultimately bring humans into contact with the sacred." This religious wave, along with the New Age Movement, is a product of Modernity which criticises the contemporary way of life that provokes alienation from nature, the stigmatisation of minorities and the marginalisation of women.

Some practitioners of Neo-paganism and Wicca have taken a more feminist connotation, presenting these new ways to express spirituality and witchcraft as a tool to enhance women's empowerment (Berger, 2005). There is a link between feminism, environmentalism, and Witchcraft, and although "not all witches or neopagans are feminist or environmentalists, many, particularly from the first wave of adherents, have incorporated elements of these movements into their beliefs and practices" (Berger, 2005). This shows how the role of witchcraft changes as a result and impacts the social context through the different eras. In every society, people search for paths to express their own spirituality, sometimes challenging the instituted forms.

The influence of feminism on witchcraft can be seen in many aspects. Traditional rituals are often reimagined to focus on feminine strength, while modern styles emphasise choice and individual empowerment over conformity to traditional practices. Some of these changes include the use of symbols, words, and rituals that focus on female energy. This shift is also reflected in the way witches are portrayed in popular culture. Gone are the days of villains lurking in dark forests ready to trap the unwary. Today, powerful women using their strength to make positive change dominate the narrative.

For many, the growing accessibility of witchcraft has created a platform for self-expression and exploration. It is stated that this is thanks to its flexibility and modernised approach, which has allowed people to find comfort within its practice. For many feminists, it has provided an opportunity to embrace their inner strength and take back control over their lives from oppressive structures. With this newfound power comes a sense of freedom—one rooted in choice and autonomy. As witches continue to gain traction in the media, it is clear that their representation is here to stay.

Chapter 5: The Spread of Witchcraft Across the Globe

As a social phenomenon, different forms of witchcraft have been present—and still are in current days—in many societies around the world and have been throughout all of history.

The proliferation of witchcraft has been moulded by a myriad of factors such as cultural exchange, colonisation, and globalisation. Witchcraft practices span diverse cultures and regions worldwide, encompassing Africa, Asia, Europe, and the Americas. Local beliefs and practices have significantly influenced these traditions, as have religious, political, and social aspects. The global exchange of ideas and beliefs has further shaped the development of witchcraft. For instance, European colonialism facilitated the exportation of European witchcraft beliefs to the Americas and Africa, where they melded with local customs and beliefs, thus giving rise to new manifestations of witchcraft.

In recent times, witchcraft has witnessed a revitalisation in popularity across various parts of the world, particularly in Western nations. This resurgence can be attributed to numerous factors, such as the growth of the New Age movement and the rising popularity of Wicca and other forms of neo-paganism. This particularly is true Western countries. A renewed interest in spiritual practices that emphasise personal empowerment and self-discovery have also played a role. Witchcraft continues to evolve and adapt in response to cultural, social, and historical forces. While the specific forms and practices of witchcraft may vary widely from one region to another, the underlying beliefs and values that motivate its practitioners remain remarkably consistent.

The European Influence

Witchcraft acquired particular nuances in Europe, where popular practices of magic played a social role in the stratified society of the Middle Ages. Most of the population were peasants, and despite the increasing hegemony of the Catholic Church as the one true faith in daily life, they were immersed in a cosmovision signed by syncretism. The figures of the cunning folk and healers coexisted with witches and sorcerers that used magic to cause harm to others. Both played an important role. While the first was the available resource for poor people to have access to healthcare, the others were rejected, excluded, and exiled. The latter represented the scapegoat for evil, social inequity, and injustice.

The understanding of witchcraft in Western mediaeval Europe later spread to other parts of the globe due to European colonial expansion that started by the end of the 15th century. It would determine changes in the so-called Old World, and would also determine the way witchcraft in other cultures was interpreted. For over three hundred years, Eurocentrism and the influence of social Darwinism led scientists to consider cultures and social organisations that deferred from European ones as less evolved, abnormal, or exotic when assuming a more benevolent perspective. This had long-term political, social, and economic consequences for the world.

The influence of Christianity gave witchcraft the singular association with maleficent practices associated with the Devil. According to Ben-Yehuda (1980), the image of the European witch before the 14th century, and the witch hunts that would then begin, had specific characteristics. These characteristics were defined according to the technology they used and the goals they pursued. Ben-Yehuda (1980) states:

> There did not yet exist developed, the systematical conceptualization of a negative supernatural world, diametrically opposed to this world and at war with it. The witch, so far, had a special position *vis-á-vis* the gods (or deities): with the correct technological use of spells, potions, and the like, she could compel them to perform specific actions (p. 3).

By the 14th century, witches became a matter of importance for the clergy. As one of the ruling estates in medieval society, the clergy created demonological theories about witchcraft that would start what is frequently called the *witch craze* (Hartigan-O'Connor, 2020). The reasons for this social phenomenon that spread, first all-over Western Europe, and later over their colonies, coincides with changes in the social structure of medieval cities and the labour market, and with the tragedy of the Black Death. In the following centuries, while the witch hunts took place (Hartigan-O'Connor, 2020),

People in Europe and its colonies in the 15th through 18th centuries believed that witches were warriors in a vast conspiracy with the devil to undermine Christian society. Common, familiar fears about witches, focused on harmful deeds (*maleficia*), were enhanced and transformed into panicked suspicion that significant numbers around the globe were signing pacts in blood with the devil to do his bidding (para. 1).

Many scholars name America the 'Atlantic World' (Hartigan-O'Connor, 2020; Breslaw, 2000) regarding the people and lands of the continent next to the Atlantic Ocean. It remained unknown to Europeans until the 15th century when Portuguese and Spanish crowns started their expeditions searching for new routes to arrive at Eastern Asia. The Portuguese first explored the Western coasts of Africa, while the Spanish fleet, led by Columbus, ventured across the ocean. In 1492, Columbus' ship arrived at the Bahamas. It was the beginning of a trading expansion and incursion of European kingdoms in lands that were inhabited by people of very different cultures. These new lands were considered by its new visitors, at that time, to be primitive.

Thus began the process of European expansion which took place between the arrival of Columbus, and the end of the 17th century. The exchange between the Europeans and the local communities brought several changes along for both groups. According to Breslaw (2000),

With trade and new settlement came the intrusion of novel ideas and traditions that in turn sometimes subtly and sometimes dramatically altered the old patterns and facilitated a usually unconscious cultural exchange. No one was immune to this transformation, neither aggressor nor victim (p. 3).

Religious practices as well as magical practices were no exception to that cultural exchange.

In the 17th century, the composition of the population in the colonies became even more diverse and complex as the enslaved people taken by European traders from the coasts of Africa were 'incorporated' into this new society. Slavery had been previously implemented by Spanish and Portuguese colonialists, subduing the native communities through different systems of exploitation: *mita* (a colonial system in Peru), *encomienda* (a slave labour system), and *yanaconazgo* (a form of servitude close to slavery). Later, Spanish clergymen reported inhuman treatment, and these forms of labour exploitation of the native population were prohibited by the laws enacted by the Spanish crown. They were replaced by African enslaved people, captured, delivered, and sold first by Portuguese traders, and later by the English, the Dutch, and the French.

Enslaved Africans brought with them their traditional practices and languages that slowly merged with other local expressions. Whether or not they were witchcraft, many of these practices, songs, dances, and rituals were perceived as magical practices and even demonic possessions. European conceptions of witchcraft conditioned their judgement over a population that was already underappreciated, and their cultural expressions were censored and persecuted.

Incorporating overseas lands into the European empires brought significant changes to the economic and social structure. The colonies played an important role not only as a provider of wealth but also as a destination to reallocate the population. The interactions between both continents—Europe and America—exceeded mere trading. The advancing of the colonisation process implied, on one hand, the shrinking and subjugation of the local communities, and on the other hand, the development of the colonial society with a strong heritage of metropolitan cultural patterns.

European settlers who immigrated to other parts of the world brought with them their own traditions and beliefs about magic and the supernatural, which eventually became part of their host countries' spiritual practices.

In Europe, witchcraft was typically associated with women, especially those on the fringes of society or with no kind of social support network. This stigma followed immigrants as they settled around the world; for example, in the United States during colonial times, accusations of witchcraft were often used against female slaves by slave owners trying to reassert control over them. In other parts of the world, such as India and Africa, practitioners of local spirituality were sometimes accused of witchcraft by Christian missionaries trying to convert them to their own belief system.

Many countries with large numbers of European settlers have adopted some aspects of native beliefs about magic and sorcery, including those associated with witches. For example, in Latin America and the Caribbean, many practices related to witchcraft draw on both Christian beliefs and traditional indigenous spiritual practices. This exemplifies how diverse religious traditions can interact with each other in meaningful ways, creating unique traditions and beliefs. It is a reminder of how fluid and ever-changing our understanding of spiritual practices can be. No matter where you look, witchcraft has left its mark on the world.

The Perspective of Witchcraft from Non-European Cultures

In the Atlantic world, witchcraft and magical thinking played important roles within communities. Breslaw (2000) considers that they replaced other ways of thinking, such as scientific discoveries and concepts of causation that provide answers to misfortune and disease. Primitive thinking would see every disaster as a result of a supernatural power's intervention: "What was universal among these societies is the belief that misfortune—whether disease, death, a loss of crops, an earthquake—came from the deliberate action of a spiritual force. Harmful events and human adversity were never accidents" (Breslaw, 2002). Therefore, there was belief in a metaphysical force with an evil power that could affect their lives.

The population in the Atlantic world at the arrival of European powers was a heterogenous scenery of languages, cultures, and socio-political organisations. Beyond that common element in their system of ideas highlighted by Breslaw, each of them identified a singular evil force. Most of them were polytheists and believed in many gods with the power to do good but also to harm and punish if individuals or communities behaved against their rules. They had established socially approved rituals to communicate with their deities, and also their own criteria to identify individuals and behaviours that acted against the conventional religious practices. According to Breslaw, these communities also had a notion of witchcraft as a practice that provoked harm by resorting to evil powers: "Calamities, if not due to a divine providence, could be traced to an evil human agent working through that invisible spiritual realm" (Breslaw, 2002). Although there were also established mechanisms to get rid of the hazardous members of the community, there is no evidence of mass persecution due to witchcraft as a crime, as there was in Europe. According to this proposal, likewise in any other societies, American native communities also accused some of their members of antisocial behaviour or using 'black magic' to harm others. Breslaw points out that they considered "witches (were) deviant people who threatened to disrupt the harmony of the community" (Breslaw, 2000). According to Breslaw, there was no fear of magical malevolence among native communities in North America. They associated misfortune with the evil actions of outsiders or their enemies, for instance, the diseases brought by the Europeans and the evil forces they embodied.

In American native communities, there were also shamans who acted in a similar way to the cunning folk in Europe. They were wise men or women, depending on the cultural group, who were able to read the nature cycle, the behaviour of animals, make predictions, and use herbs with the power to heal. As it was explained in the chapter covering shamanism, there are some meaningful differences between shamans and cunning folk. While the first performed in public, occupied a powerful position within the internal structure and were feared by the community, the others performed privately, were marginal subjects, and were sometimes feared and rejected by society, and later persecuted for their practices (Breslaw, 2020; Singh, 2020).

Even though many common elements can be found between witchcraft beliefs and practices on both sides of the Atlantic Ocean, there are fundamental differences. In Christian traditions, there is an idea of evil forces that are opposed and act against God—the only source of good, and incapable of causing harm. Therefore, if there were individuals with the ability to harm, it necessarily had to be related to the Devil, the source of evil. Mediaeval Christians sustained the idea of a "God as a benevolent and omniscient being, ready to help his believers. (…) Evil itself was promoted by a lesser force called Satan, a devil, a ruler of darkness who was determined to overthrow the true deity by subverting his kingdom on earth"

(Breslaw, 2000). Any supernatural force acting on earth to harm or cause disgrace could be nothing but an act of witchcraft and the use of dark powers.

When it comes to understanding witchcraft in African communities, scholars face the obstacle of lack of sufficient research and register of these types of practices (Mesaki, 1995). The most agreed versions affirm that witchcraft merges with other religious and cultural practices which are difficult to distinguish. However, Western scientific research on African witchcraft cannot avoid the Christian bias on its connotation.

Mesaki (1995) retrieves several pieces of research to analyse witchcraft practices in Africa. It is considered that in the early Iron Age, some communities "had acquired a set of beliefs which attributed evil mostly to human malice and envy," deviating social conflicts to individual behaviour inspired by personal malevolence (Mesaki, 1995).

According to Mesaki's sources, there are two currents for scholars in African witchcraft studies to be considered. The first, considers that witchcraft became important after the process of sedentarisation when societies began to differentiate. The second, associates witchcraft with the European slavery trade development (Mesaki, 1995). The source Mesaki consulted explains pre-colonial Calabar—southern Nigeria—that witchcraft was a way to relieve social tension triggered by a new internal segmentation: those with a privileged traditional status, and those with a privileged position due to the trade (Mesaki, 1995).

According to Breslaw's collection of scholarly research on witchcraft in African cultures, there is a belief in evil forces that can act through a human agent in a similar way to the European version. Additionally, the agent can be male or female instinctively. Therefore, "Africans rely on other magical rituals to protect themselves against the evil that causes suffering or turn to oracles, divination tools, to identify the evildoers, who can then be punished" (Breslaw, 2000). The African enslaved people brought with them their original cultural traditions, and these practices, to the European colonies in America.

In the 16th and 17th centuries, native people in America and Africa believed that the world was not only settled by material beings but also of spirits of dead people that continued to live in another dimension. They thought spirits were responsible for all the suffering and adversity. Breslaw retrieves works that affirm that, in Africa, there coexisted two types of witches, those that were able to face spirits that menaced the community, and those dedicated to causing harm. Introduced as slaves in the American communities, their beliefs were based on the fear of ghosts and spirits of the dead. They believed these entities from the parallel world returned to take revenge for ancient offences that were common among the colonies.

Scholars argue that some witchcraft ideas and magical explanations of diseases and death were brought by the African enslaved people to America. Others, instead, consider that many enslaved persons embraced American people and their ideas about witchcraft, although they did have previous knowledge about the use of herbs to heal, as well as to harm. This knowledge was the property of the *obia*, or witch doctor—from a European perspective. However, there was a specific practice that the enslaved certainly carried with them and brought into the colonies. This practice was divination. As Breslaw (2020) puts it:

> This was the traditional function of the oracle in Africa. The belief in magical divining was especially effective as a psychological device used by Africans in America to identify criminals and thus a method of reducing conflict within their own black communities, both slaves and free. (p. 100).

Both population components in the colonies, American native people and the enslaved Africans could only continue their cultural and religious practices under adverse life conditions. American native people were forced to convert to Christianism and leave aside their ancient beliefs and practices. According to Redden (2013), most Africans didn't know much about Europeans and certainly did not understand their language. Many testimonies render that they received a flying baptism—the Christian ceremony to erase the original sin and make the person a son of God—before being thrown into the slave ship to cross the ocean toward the colonies. Many of them would die after days of subhuman and unhealthy conditions, and be thrown into the sea. Redden affirms that many Africans found a relationship between the ritual of baptism. Some gave it a positive connotation as a remedy for illnesses. Others fearing that it was an invention of the witches, and "sometimes thought that baptism was a spell that enabled the Spanish to eat them or even turn them into gunpowder."

In some African cultures, the ritual of death is seen as a transformative process in which the deceased are guided into the afterlife by ancestral spirits or other supernatural forces. Similarly, the experience of being taken away by European slave traders was often framed as a journey into the unknown, where the enslaved were forced to confront new and unfamiliar circumstances that challenged their sense of identity, community, and purpose. Redden points out that Africans first thought that these white people coming from over the sea were visitors from the land of the dead. In a similar way, in America, the natives that met Columbus and his crew on their first trip, initially welcomed them since they believed these white people with strange attires were the gods' emissaries. The Portuguese that arrived at the coasts of Congo and gave the imprisoned locals a flying baptism were seen as "dead white priests" and "might easily have been considered the ghostly counterparts of witches who were condemned to wander the infertile grasslands and attack and eat the living" (Redden, 2013). From the African perspective, this could have been a confirmation that power could be obtained through witchcraft. Those who survived the journey toward the colonies would find out that this ritual was indeed the announcement of misfortune.

Both native Americans and the enslaved Africans living under the colonial yoke created ways to express their fears and process the misfortune of their communities in different ways. Most of them as a result of syncretic processes. There are several archaeological sites that have revealed rituals, including artefacts and dolls. These, at first sight, were interpreted as magical practices with intent to harm. However, it has not been confirmed that this was their original purpose. All along the American territory, scientists have found artefacts which have been called manikins. It is actually believed that these objects may have been used for medical purposes, or indeed divination.

European settlers who arrived in the Atlantic world and encountered unfamiliar witchcraft practices attempted to make sense of these occurrences within their own worldviews. This approach often led to a distorted interpretation of indigenous spiritual customs and rituals, resulting in suspicion and fear among the settlers.

For example, many Europeans believed Native Americans were pagans who practised devil worship and thus posed a threat to Christian society. As a result, they sought to eradicate such perceived dangers by attempting to convert the Indigenous peoples to Christianity, as well as punishing those suspected of practising traditional witchcraft with death or imprisonment.

European colonists often misunderstood various aspects of the Native American beliefs such as sacred ceremonies involving plants or animals. To them, these rituals were seen as "superstitious" and associated with the Devil. The European interpretation of the Atlantic world's practices ultimately resulted in a wide range of misinformed assumptions that were based on fear rather than understanding. Such misinterpretations had far-reaching consequences for both the indigenous peoples and settlers alike, as it caused an increased mistrust between them and contributed to a legacy of violence against those suspected of practising traditional customs.

The European Interpretation of the Atlantic World's Witchcraft Practices

People's beliefs are not totally rational and conscious. Instead, they are shaped and determined by the cultural background that mediates the comprehension of the world that surrounds them. In this way, the American and African local communities interpreted Europeans arriving to their lands in correspondence with their current cosmovision and system of beliefs. Similarly, Europeans observed the New World through the lenses of their cultural bias. Therefore, most of the registers and writings about the Americans' and Africans' practices are misunderstood as distorted descriptions from people who were trying to make all those practices fit within their own system of ideas (Breslaw, 2000). This has prevented historians, anthropologists, and sociologists from having access to accurate sources of information that clearly interpret their worldviews and spiritual practices.

There were several common components that Europeans, Native Americans, and Africans shared regarding the influence of supernatural forces acting over the destiny of human beings. This included the view of evil, acting through human agents, as the cause for misfortune. Breslaw (2000) points out that on both sides of the Atlantic, witchcraft and the evil use of magic were attributed to people exhibiting antisocial behaviour, in conflict with the community's harmony. This would provide the motivation for others to harm them.

Despite these intersections among the different cultures, Europeans were entrenched in another explanation for the evil in the material world, which could not be attributed to a benevolent god. For the mediaeval Christian tradition of the 15th century, when the European expansion began, all magical rituals were associated with evil. Christian religious practices involved human agents that mediated with supernatural forces. They—the priests—interpreted the divine words, and were the only ones qualified to talk to God. Especially during the late Middle Ages, and before the Protestant Reformation. The rituals and the sacred scriptures were privately and exclusively performed by the clergy—the parishioners having a very passive role in them. Catholic practitioners also had their own symbols and rituals, with sacred places to perform them. However, any ritual or similar practices outside the Christian paradigm were considered heresy by European theologians.

As it will be covered in the following chapter, the construction of the concept of witchcraft in Europe to be a manifestation of evil, caused the onset of the "The Witch Craze". This developed into the hunt and subsequent trials of people—mostly women—accused of witchcraft. This phenomenon coincided with a complex gathering of social, political, and economic changes and a revolution of ideas. Altogether, this complex

European scenery was conveyed to the continents that were included in the known world. Incorporating the colonies and the process of colonisation of the new territories provoked mutual influence among all the cultures involved. The way that European colonists understood, or misunderstood, the native practices was heavily influenced by what was happening in the motherland. Even the legal framework from Europe was transplanted from Europe to America, advocating similar judgements and sentencing.

Many scholars highlight the registers and testimonies by Europeans on the local religious practices. Those that were considered witchcraft retrieved all the cultural nuances of the shared characterisation of witchcraft founded in Europe. In fact, many of the testimonies and allegations against those accused of witchcraft in America repeated the same ideology of Europe.

Delores E. Wren

Chapter 6: Witch Hunts Throughout History

The belief in witches and their ability to harm people through magical means, started what is now known as the "witch hunts". These hunts were, and still are, in certain parts of the world, the persistent and extensive persecution of those who were suspected of practising witchcraft. Witch hunts and trials throughout history have been a significant and tragic phenomenon, characterised by oppression, maltreatment and often violent punishment of the accused. They have occurred in many different cultures and time periods, and have often been motivated by a combination of religious and social factors. One of the primary reasons for witch hunts has been, quite simply, irrational fear.

Accusations of witchcraft were often made in times of crisis or social unrest, as people sought to identify and punish those they believed were responsible for their troubles. In many cases, accusations of witchcraft were used to suppress dissent by punishing individuals who were seen as a threat to the established religious or social norm.

The Witch Craze

The Western Europe conception of witchcraft that has already been explained, resulted from the social and economic changes that took place in the continent. According to Ben-Yehuda (1980), the traditional ideas of witchcraft, retrieving Weber's contributions, was a kind of technology used for specific goals and serving human needs. This conception began to change in the 14th century. At this time, there was a transformation of the general context. It caused, as a result of what is now called the witch craze, the mass persecution, and execution of thousands of people, who were accused of witchcraft between the 14th and the 17th centuries. Most of them were women. This is a phenomenon that only took place at a specific period, in a specific part of the world. While witchcraft practices can be found in almost every culture studied by sociologists and anthropologists, there is no clear evidence of witches being hunted in the way they were in Europe. Even though people feared witches and wizards, only the Western Europeans developed an entire legal system to imprison and execute people for witchcraft.

Ben-Yehuda (1980) affirms that this phenomenon can be explained by understanding the demographic and economic changes, and other circumstances that took place in Europe, in the late Middle Ages and in early Modernity. The answer can be found, in particular, during the 14th century. According to the author, "the witch craze answered the need for a redefinition of moral boundaries, as a result of the profound changes in the medieval social order" (Ben-Yehuda, 1980, p.1). The Black Death (1346 to 1353.) caused a demographic catastrophe. It provoked the death of two-thirds of the European population. This caused a deep moral crisis that triggered an increase in the hunting of witches.

The Protestant Reformation of 1517—a political and religious process of separation of the Catholic Church—contributed to the deepening of the moral crisis of the time. The Thirty Years' War that took place between 1618 and 1648 in central Europe, but affected most of the regions of the continent, increased the hardship of the population further. The centuries of crop failure caused widespread famine among a population dependent on agriculture. Two more plagues scourged the weakened communities. It is not so hard to imagine why the faith of the people was hesitant, and vulnerable to generalised social paranoia.

The witch craze was a two-level phenomenon. First, the established powers, especially the Catholic Church, and on the second, the popular reaction of accusing people of witchcraft. Some theories consider the witch hunts were a scapegoat for a global crisis—the lack of consistent moral principles, a crisis of faith due to the death caused by a pandemic, constant wars, and poverty all adding to the mix. All of this, accompanied by economic changes and the transformation of daily life for a population of peasants who had to move from the country to the villages. Other theories emphasise the importance and intensity of the religious phenomenon, and how it was so deliberately constructed.

The concern for witchcraft and witches had begun in the 13th century when the Catholic Church created the Inquisition, an institution with the purpose of ensuring the hegemony of Christianism as the only and true religion. The characteristics and roles of this institution will be explained in the following sections. While in its origins it pursued heretics, from the 14th century on, the focus was almost entirely on witchcraft.

There is no conclusive evidence of the total number of people who were hunted and executed after being accused of witchcraft. The research carried out by Gendercide (n.d.), affirms that there were "40,000 to 50,000 witch executions in Europe between 1450 and 1750, and an estimated 75%-80% of those executed were women." Men were also accused of witchcraft, but the significant majority of women were conditioned to think that there were specific conditions that made them the preferred target. According to Ben-Yehuda (1980), this can be explained by framing the phenomenon in the process of subversion of the medieval social order. This reverted the social roles of people, but the roles of women were particularly affected.

During the 13th century, advances in the general production processes began to increase in the Low Countries and England, and from there, spread to the region of the Rhine. The cities began to gain more importance, spreading and attracting the population. This resulted in economic development, population increase, and the appearance of a distinct way of life from the traditional peasant life in the fields and villages that characterised the Middle Ages. The social division of work was simple, and the role of women was limited to domestic responsibilities. This mostly involved helping their husbands in the harvest, and especially giving birth and raising children. This was a period in history, when life expectancy was low, and survival depended upon the number of people available to work in the fields to provide for their families and wider community. Having children and keeping them alive was of the utmost importance.

The families that used to live in rural communities, made their lives from the land, and produced for self-subsistence. Many of them had to move from the country to the cities. The new rhythm of life and the new logic of production, now for the market, represented a deep change in these people. Their new found perspective on life had a great impact on them, in particular for the women.

With the expansion of industrial production and commerce, the cities increased the standardisation and specialisation of jobs, and deepened the division of labour. The hierarchical structure of medieval society collapsed. Despite the increase in economic activity and money in circulation, the new citizens working in the former industries had very low incomes. The number of marriages also began to decrease. Proportionally, the number of women who lacked the possibility to enter society to fulfil the role they had been assigned increased. This situation posed two types of pressure for women. They were forced to enter the labour market not having other means to survive. This often prevented them from assuming the expected roles of wives and mothers. According to several scholarly research sources retrieved by Ben-Yehuda (1980), a high number of witch-hunt cases coincided with regions where this economic and social process of change had taken place.

In the late Middle Ages and early Modernity, many women were expelled from the social system and became a matter of suspicion. A view formed—if they were not complying with the rules that society had shaped for them, then they must be taking part in immoral or illegal activities.

The Papal Inquisition

The Papal Inquisition became a group of institutions that was established by the Roman Catholic Church in 1231. The power of the Catholic Church was in the spiritual and ideological fundamentals of a hierarchical social system. It was embedded in a cosmic order, centred on God. The Inquisition was the way the Catholic Church tried to preserve that hegemony from the social and political changes that were occurring in Europe. Prior to 1231, there were isolated practices carried out by bishops and regional clergy authorities. Then, Pope Gregory IX delegated the execution of the Inquisition to the Dominican and Franciscan orders (Hamilton & Peters, 2022). Previously, they lacked the formal authority or guidance. When the Inquisitorial Book of Practice was written in the 13th century, all inquisitors used similar procedures and had the full force of the church behind them.

The Inquisition's objective was to combat heresy. This was achieved by applying judicial inquiries to determine, judge, and condemn it. According to the dictionary, heresy is the "adherence to a religious opinion contrary to church dogma" (Merriam-Webster, n.d.), but also the "denial of a revealed truth by a baptised member of the Roman Catholic Church" (Merriam-Webster, n.d.). Indeed, the Catholic Church considered all religious practices that denied or deviated from its beliefs as heresy. Previously, the focus of heresy had been upon the Arians and Manicheans. In the Middle Ages it fell upon the Cathari and the Waldensians. Then, in the early Modernity, after the Protestant Reformation, it became the turn of the Hussites, the Lutherans, the Calvinists and the Rosicrucians. At the same time, the presence of Jews and Muslims was perceived to be a threat to the Catholic Church's power. The Inquisition's procedures carried out were concentrated in France, Italy, and Germany. Spain also implemented judicial inquiries and even spread the practice to its colonies in America. In general, the objective of the Inquisition was to make the heretics renounce their sinful practices, convert to Catholicism, and beg for redemption.

The usual procedure consisted of the institution of an inquiry within a certain jurisdiction. It was here that the inquisitor would establish a period of grace to allow the accused to voluntarily confess crimes of heresy. This was expected to produce a more lenient punishment or penance. The inquisitors then added to and built up a list of more suspects based on these confessions. They could then accuse those on these lists without any further testimonies or evidence required. The inquiries and interrogations were carried out only by the inquisitor and a notary that recorded the testimonies. The accused had no right to defend themselves with a lawyer, or any who could advocate for them. The suspect also did not have the right to know who had accused them, or what the evidence against them was. Even though the accused appealed to the pope to intervene in the procedure, it was an expensive formality that most of the accused were unable to afford.

There has been a lot of research and historical evidence found into torture practices that were employed by the inquisitors to obtain a confession. Hamilton and Peters (2022) point out that,

> In 1252, Pope Innocent IV licensed inquisitors to allow obdurate heretics to be tortured by lay henchmen. It is difficult to determine how common this practice was in the 13th century, but the inquisition certainly acquiesced in the use of torture in the trial of the Knights Templar, a military-religious order, in 1307 (p. 2).

The accused would remain imprisoned and isolated while the judicial procedure was being carried out. The sentences of those found guilty of heresy were exposed in the public homily. Those who admitted their crimes would receive religious penances, the stigma of a yellow cross as the symbol of a converted heretic, or time in prison. Those who refused to confess were condemned to be burnt at the stake at the hands of secular authorities. The Church confiscated all the properties of the accused to cover the expenses of the trial. Families of the victims were deprived and dishonoured.

These inquiries for heresy were a precedent for the witch trials that took place from the 14th century onwards. The theologians of the Inquisition provided the theological and conceptual framework to identify witches, to fear them, and to hunt them. Over time, the Inquisition expanded its reach and became a powerful institution throughout much of Europe. The Inquisition also played a significant role in the Spanish Reconquista (8th century until 1492) and the forced conversion of Jews and Muslims to Christianity.

While the Inquisition officially ended in the 19th century, its legacy has continued to shape the Catholic Church and European societies more broadly. Today, the Church has acknowledged the harm that the Inquisition caused. They have also expressed regret for the suffering it caused to countless individuals over the centuries. The Inquisition remains a part of history that is often used as an allegory for unchecked authority or oppressive power. Its legacy casts a long shadow over modern society. It serves as a reminder that faith should never be imposed on others. It should instead be embraced with respect and understanding. In recognition of this important lesson, many countries around the world have abolished laws that seek to punish people for their religious beliefs. Sadly, not all.

Historical and Religious Perspectives on Witch Hunts

The Catholic Church went through a process of internal transformation that ended with the institution's separation into two branches. In 1517, Martin Luther led a protest against the corruption within the Catholic Church in the current territories of Germany. He raised his voice against the sale of indulgences that Pope X offered to the parishioners—the offer to release souls in purgatory in exchange for money. This money was destined for the Church. Later, for his views, Luther was excommunicated and received a death sentence. However, political issues intervened and princes from the kingdoms that formed the Holy Roman Empire gave him protection. In France, John Calvin followed Luther's resistance and rejection of the authority of the Roman Catholic Church. He founded a new Christian religious branch that did not recognise the pope's power.

Luther and Calvin started the Protestant Reformation, posing an alternative practice of the Christian faith outside the borders of the Catholic institutions. It encouraged people to live their faith more as a personal practice, as well as the reading of the Bible. This process added to the political instability of Central Europe. Now the persecution of the heretics became merged with political reasons as well. In response, the Catholic Church began the process of Counter-Reformation.

The process of separation of the Catholic Church created many problems. The emergence of new practices questioned the central and unique authority that had dominated Europe for more than a thousand years. This was a new source of conflict. The propaganda, carried out by the Protestants to spread their faith, was also a factor that contributed to deepening the witch craze. According to Breslaw (2000), the non-Catholic churches that emerged due to the Reformation were eager to convert the partially Christianised population who continued to practice folk rituals.

In reverse, the Catholic Counter-Reformation found in the Protestants parishioners new heretics to persecute and eradicate, associating their ideas with Satan. This conflict took place in the religious realm and had its counterpart in the political dispute: "Political leaders may have found the Inquisition and witch trials in local courts useful means of getting rid of their secular oppositions, but the religious justification, the urge to combat the devil, provided the moral force" (Breslaw, 2000). This shows how the conception, or rather the created misconception of witchcraft, was used to repress and exclude those who chose to step against the established order or to face and fight it. This is also an indication of how spiritual ideas and popular manifestation had been used to subdue and control the population for the benefit of the established powers. Here, the idea of good and evil, of moral and immoral were used as social control weapons.

Historians have argued that many mediaeval Europeans viewed witchcraft as an insidious force—one that could not simply be eradicated by punishing its practitioners. Instead, they believed it was necessary to prevent, or rather, eliminate its spread, by the use of cruel punishments which included execution. The hysteria that ensued caused people to accuse their neighbours or family members of witchcraft. This led to further widespread paranoia and mistrust.

As beliefs in witchcraft dwindled during the Enlightenment period, witch hunts began to decline. Today, there is a much greater understanding and appreciation for the historical significance of these events. They are however, still remembered with a sense of dread and caution. It has been impossible to gauge the true extent of these tragedies. What remains clear is that they had a devastating impact on those who were accused. This impact continues to reverberate through history even today.

It is important to note that although witch hunts were primarily driven by religious and political motives, there was also a general deep-seated fear of women. In the majority, they were targeted by the witch hunters. Women were perceived as being more vulnerable to the supernatural forces that drove many of these hunts. As a result, they were seen as potential threats and sources of evil. It is this legacy of fear and mistrust—fuelled by religious and cultural beliefs—that has haunted witches for centuries. Despite progress in understanding the historical significance of witch hunts, there is still much work to be done in order to prevent such events from occurring again. Though the practice of witch hunts is largely viewed as anachronistic today, there are cultures which still view women with suspicion due to their alleged connection to witchcraft. Unfortunately, for some, the trials continue.

The Malleus Maleficarum

In the 15th century, an invention changed the course of history—Johannes Gutenberg invented the printing press. This became a significant tool for the spread of new ideas, opening the path for the revolution of scientific knowledge and popular education. The first book that the press was used to publish was the Bible. This played a significant role in the spread of the Protestant Reformation, which eventually provoked internal and external changes in the Catholic Church. On one hand, this helped to bring the sacred text of the bible to all people. On the other hand, the printing press was used to spread the message of fear and hatred that fed the social panic regarding witchcraft. Along with the Bible, the most popular publications were witch-hunting manuals (Farrell et al., n.d.). There was one infamous witch-hunting book in particular—The *Malleus Maleficarum*. Published in 1486, no one could have quite predicted the impact it would have.

At that time, the moral boundaries that dominated mediaeval society based on Christian principles had lost legitimacy, and the Catholic Church's power was weakened. Therefore, it needed an opponent to regain relevance and recover authority. As stated in the previous chapter, in Germany—where the authority of the Catholic Church felt most threatened—Protestant Reformation took place.

Heinrich Kramer, an Inquisitor from the Catholic Church, was the author of the Malleus Maleficarum. The Catholic Church however, never officially assumed the responsibility for its publication. Also known as the "Hammer of the Witches", this book argued that witchcraft was real and presented arguments to support these views. The arguments were based on superstition, religious ideology, and folklore. It represented the institutionalisation of witchcraft as the embodiment of evil, and the conception of witches as the nexus between Satan and mortals. Until then, there was no previous systematisation of witchcraft and its practices. There was not something to be called the ideology of evil in opposition to Christianity. The Malleus Maleficarum was an alarming success in Europe and went through 28 editions by 1669. Church-sanctioned witch hunts swept across Europe. People followed its instructions on how to prosecute witches, and countless innocent women were accused and persecuted.

Pope Innocent VIII had emitted a papal bull, the *'Summis desiderantes affectibus'* a few years earlier, before Kramer wrote the Malleus. He had promoted the persecution of religious minorities accused of heresy, and with the bull, he delivered an official recognition of the existence of witches. This bull and its dispositions were included in the *Malleus* and gave the Dominicans the authorisation to accuse and pursue people for witchcraft (Deyrmenjian, 2020). Any religious practice outside the Catholic Church and its rituals, or any other religious reading or expression, was not just considered as heresy. It now became a crime.

The Malleus Maleficarum was a manual used by both inquisitors and common people to identify and accuse those who practised witchcraft. Although it was the most widespread and had the acquiescence of Pope Innocence, there were at least 15 books written and published about when, where, and how to recognise a witch (Ben-Yehuda, 1980). The manual provided a detailed description of witches and their practices, and most of it was aimed at women (Ben-Yehuda, 1980; Stringer, 2015). The book had an explicit misogynist tone: According to Mederos (2020),

> In the opening passage of the manual, Kramer declares women to be the sole operators of witchcraft, exclaiming, "What else is woman but a foe to friendship, an inescapable punishment, a necessary evil, a natural temptation, a desirable calamity, a domestic danger, a delectable detriment, an evil of nature, painted with fair colors" (p. 1).

According to Mederos' (2020) research, gender stereotypes and prejudice played a central role in the Malleus Maleficarum, which in fact reflected the ideas from the time and the social environment.

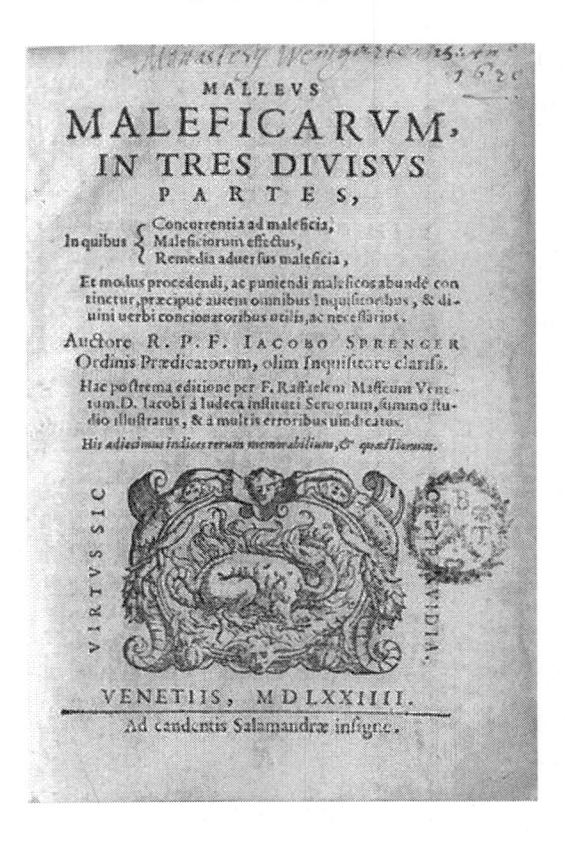

Figure 10: Title page of an edition of the Malleus Maleficarum (The Hammer of Witches), Venice 1574; from the library of the Weingarten Monastery. Unknown author, Public domain, via Wikimedia Commons (https://commons.wikimedia.org/wiki/File:Hexenhammer_Weingarten. jpg)

The book was divided into three parts:

The first part dealt with the initial allegation to prove the existence of witches and their relationship with the Devil. At the time, most people tended to believe either witchcraft was harmless, or that it didn't even exist. The purpose of the Malleus was to convince people of the real power of witchcraft, and the threat it meant for them, and for the Church.

The second part described the signs, behaviours, and activities that characterised a witch. Also, the necessary tests and inspections to recognise them. According to the Malleus, witches performed pacts and interacted with the Devil. The Malleus Maleficarum also contained and detailed the new concept of the witches' Sabbath rituals. According to the book, witches would gather in secret at night to perform rituals and engage in various acts of debauchery and blasphemy. The Malleus describes the witches' Sabbath in great detail, including the supposed presence of demons. The Malleus also played a role in popularising the idea of witches flying on broomsticks or other objects. The book claims that witches would anoint themselves with a special ointment that would allow them to fly to the Sabbath. Descriptions were provided on how witches would apply the ointment to their bodies, along with the use of broomsticks or other objects to aid in their flight.

The third part of the book explained why it was legitimate and obligatory to carry out the investigation and prosecution of those who practised witchcraft. The procedures included torture and execution if the accused refused to confess and relinquish the demoniac beliefs.

Although the Malleus Maleficarum was not the only book about witchcraft, it was certainly the most disseminated book of its type in Europe. The book had at least 20 editions and had a great impact on priests and other religious magistrates. The inclusion of the *Summis desiderantes affectibus* released any legal obstructions. This then allowed the Dominicans and the rest of the clergy to hunt and prosecute people suspected of witchcraft with impunity. It represented the beginning of witch hunting. Although many of the people accused of witchcraft would eventually confess their crimes—undoubtedly due to the atrocious torture that was posed to them—the popular fear of witches increased exponentially.

The manual standardised people's beliefs of witchcraft. Even those accused of it tended to repeat what was expected from a witch. Therefore, all the testimonies alleging witchcraft and also confessions were similar. Broedel (2003) explains that "the Malleus, in other words, proposed a basic shift in how the Church should conceptualise evil, a shift which not all contemporaries were prepared to accept." The ideas and dispositions established by the Malleus Maleficarum were used in all of Europe. It was later taken to the colonies.

According to the manual, there were two main witchcraft practices to be eradicated. First, the performance of the maleficium, and second, diabolism or worship of the Devil. The idea that witchcraft was a type of heresy was already popular during the Middle Ages, but it was formally included as a heresy crime from the 15th century onwards (Broedel, 2003). The use of magic, either witchcraft or sorcery, became characterised as heresy as they were associated with demonic forces, despite the objectives of the magicians. With the Malleus Maleficarum, every magical practice, including the traditional magical spells popular among the peasants, was considered a practice of maleficium, harmful magic that involved the invocation of evil forces (Broedel, 2003). The theologists agreed in affirming that there were only two possible sources of power in the universe: God and the Devil. If there were people who invoked supernatural forces and it wasn't by the means of Christian rituals and words, then it was witchcraft, therefore, again, heresy.

Then, Catholic theorists proposed the theory that witches owed their power from having made a pact with the Devil. Stringer (2015) analyses the Malleus Maleficarum and affirms that "during the early modern period, witchcraft was a crime not only because of the harm involved in *maleficia* or *malicious* magical acts, but more importantly, it was an act of apostasy as witches supposedly renounced God and worshipped the Devil. The accusations of worship of the Devil were developed alongside the idea of the witches' Sabbath.

The book provided instructions on how to eliminate witches. One method was to submerge them into freezing water. But also, this was a method to uncover witches who would not confess. It consisted in stripping the woman accused of witchcraft and throwing her into a body of water. If the woman floated, then it meant that the waters rejected her because she had been marked by the Devil. If she sank, then she would then be considered innocent. Even though most of the women floated, many of them simply drowned. This method was called "swimming the witch" and it was more used in Eastern Europe during its period of the witch craze, but also in Western Europe.

Then, there was a further accusation described in the Malleus of how witches subverted the order of nature: cannibalism. Stringer (2015) points out that the accusations relied upon arguments on how practitioners of witchcraft subverted the relationship with the supernatural, but also all the social conventions: "Cannibalism is, of course, a devastating inversion of social norms, and the witch, like the heretic, was constructed to be the embodiment of anti-social vice and deviance." These accusations of witchcraft proliferated in the turbulent society of central Europe as it was entering Modernity.

The Great Witch Hunt

According to Lambert (2022), the witch hunts began in the 14th and 15th centuries in Central Europe. Later, it spread to the United Kingdom in the 16th century, arriving at the Scandinavian peninsula in the last stage of the process, in the 17th century. In countries with a weaker central authority, such as France, Switzerland, and Germany, there was often no strong legal system in place to regulate the prosecution of witchcraft. This meant that accusations of witchcraft were often left to local communities to handle, which could result in a more extreme and unregulated response. In Spain and Portugal, where Catholicism was stronger, it focused upon the Jews and Muslims as the main target for the Inquisition trials. In the Iberian Peninsula, the accusations of heresy prevailed over witchcraft

(Ben-Yehuda, 1980). The witch craze was less intense in England, Northern Europe, and Russia (Lambert, 2022).

In general, the prosecution of the judicial trials against people accused of witchcraft followed the instructions of the Inquisition manuals. The use of torture was one reason witch hunts and witchcraft accusations increased so rapidly. The prosecutors were able to use torture methods in order to obtain a confession from the accused. Many people would give away the name of family members, neighbours or indeed familiars to stop the suffering. This resulted in more and more victims being accused. Subsequently expanding the extent of witch hunting and providing the fuel to deeper the witch craze. (Hunt, 2022).

It is called the Great Witch Hunt because of the series of trials put on people accused of witchcraft (Hunt, 2022). The trials were preceded by long judicial procedures carried out by the inquisitorial powers and then passed to the secular powers. The procedure deprived the accused of any sort of rights and was carried out in secrecy. The inquisitor authorities played a central role in the trial's outcome. Besides, "the placement of witchcraft trials in local and secular courts enabled the Great European Witch Hunt, as local authorities who were more likely to fear witchcraft and abuse the system were backed by the full judicial power of the state" (Hunt, 2022).

Protestants also carried out witch hunts and trials, not only in Europe, but also in the territories of the colonies beyond the sea. Although they were not a part of the Catholic church hierarchy, the protestants acknowledged the need to follow the catholic procedures regarding witchcraft. They endorsed the secret judicial processes and the public executions as a confirmation of the morality and legitimacy of the new protestant teachings.

The witch craze also exposed the vulnerability of the more marginalised members of European society. In particular, those who were female, poor, or had a lower social status often became targets for false accusations. The role of gender in this period cannot be overstated. Women were seen as inherently more likely to engage in witchcraft than men and thus received harsher punishments than their male counterparts when found guilty.

The end of the witch craze was supported by the new changes in the political scenario and in the intellectual realm. The end of the Thirty Years' War in the middle of the century represented a new era in the organisation of the state powers in central Europe. This ended the long years of political instability. The shakeup of the Reformation and the Counter-Reformation processes also had settled down and social unrest had decreased.

In addition, the Enlightenment provided a new framework for progress in rational debate, which helped to combat the witch craze. It encouraged people to question traditional beliefs and seek evidence to support or refute claims of witchcraft. The rise of science and advancements in technology also provided people with better tools for understanding, which helped to establish a more evidence-based approach to understanding the world.

The modernisation of secular states assisted the development of legal systems that kept justice under the secular powers by removing it from the ecclesiastical authorities. These new legal secular systems abolished the hunting of witches. Slowly, states became more stable, and Europe went through a stage of economic security that would help to reduce social hysteria. Paranoia, regarding witchcraft, declined. In the following two centuries, social unrest would be driven by new political ideas.

Chapter 7: The Witch Trials in Europe

Throughout the previous chapters, we have looked upon the European Influence of Witchcraft. In this chapter, we will take a closer look at Europe itself and how witchcraft acquired these particular connotations, which were later spread all over the world through European expansion.

Continental Europe - A Quick History Lesson

Understanding the history of continental Europe and its beginnings is critical when discussing the history of witchcraft in this region. In doing so, it helps to contextualise the beliefs and practices of its people during this period. It's history sheds light on the complex social, economic, and religious factors that shaped how witchcraft evolved, how it was viewed and understood.

It is not correct to refer to Europe as a whole because Europe is comprised of many different countries with distinct cultures, histories, and political systems. Each country has its own unique identity, language, and customs that differentiate it from the others. Therefore, it would be inaccurate to assume that all of Europe shares the same beliefs, values, or attitudes. For instance, we have previously used the concept of Western Europe, which implies that there is an Eastern Europe. This refers to the portion of the continent that remained under the power of the Eastern Roman Empire, which lasted until 1453. This was almost a millennium more than the Western Roman

Empire, which had fallen into the hands of the Goth invaders. The Eastern Roman Empire had Istanbul as its capital, and it occupied the Balkan Peninsula, the Arabian Peninsula, and other Asian and North-Western African territories. It had a totally different evolution from the Western part of the continent. In 1453, the Ottomans took control and imposed their culture, law, religion and way of life.

Western Europe became a fusion of the Roman Empire's cultural legacy and the influence of several Germanic races that had infiltrated the empire's borders since the 3rd century. The Roman Empire had previously merged its culture and practices with the ancient native people in Europe: Celtic, Gauls, Lusitanos, Anglos, and the Saxons. In the 4th century, Christianity became the official religion of the empire. Existing religious practices were inherited from these races that were impossible to eradicate. In fact, Christianism merged with many of the pagan practices and were adopted in their rituals.

Later, between the 4th and the 5th century, Germanic people from Central and Northern Europe came into the Roman Empire. This process would eventually precipitate the fall of these people. The Germanic tribes were the Franks, the Goths (Visigoths and Ostrogoths), the Vandali, the Burgundian, the Teutons, and many others (Kessler & Dawson, n.d.). They brought into Roman domains their languages, their ideas about life and death, their deities, religious practices, and their knowledge of nature. Later, the Normans, the Vikings, the Magyars, and the Saracens also arrived and the cultural intermingling continued to deepen. In the first centuries after the fall of the Western Roman Empire (476), the Germanic tribes settled in different parts of Europe. They built Roman-Germanic monarchies, a blended social, cultural, and political system that retrieved components of both cultural groups. Many of the Roman-Germanic monarchs converted from their original Arianism and other religions to Catholicism.

Later, during the medieval and early modern periods, the Catholic Church's influence in Europe was immense, and its teachings and beliefs had a significant impact on the way people thought about witchcraft. Furthermore, the Catholic Church's influence on continental Europe extended beyond the persecution of witches. Its teachings on morality, sin, and redemption shaped the beliefs and practices of many people during this period.

Witchcraft Trials in Central Europe

Nitschke (2022) talks about the most emblematic witch trials in Central Europe: the first systematic European witch hunt took place in Valais, a Swiss canton, in 1428. The prosecution accused and subsequently executed 367 people over an eight year period. The procedure to condemn demanded at least three witnesses that could confirm that the accused was guilty of witchcraft. The witch hunt of Valais targeted mostly male peasants who were tortured to extract confessions. Many confessions coincided with admitting to meeting with the Devil and obtaining the ability to fly or to turn into an animal. Most of them were sentenced to die at the stake, whilst others were beheaded.

Figure 11: Within the walls of the Rila Monastery in Bulgaria, a profound painting stands as a condemnation of witchcraft and the practices of traditional folk magic. Public Domain via Wikimedia Commons (https://commons.wikimedia.org/wiki/File:Rila_Monastery_wall_pain ting.jpg)

Germany

Germany is often noted as being the epicentre of the witch craze. One of the most terrible witch hunts took place in Bamberg, Germany. Between 1626 to 1631, a thousand people, men, and women of all ages, were accused and prosecuted for witchcraft. 900 of them were condemned to die at the stake. Some of them were beheaded first and then burned. This case illustrates, yet again, how social hysteria led to massive trials.

This began when some peasants accused their neighbours of ruining their crops by witchcraft. Since this process admitted many extreme forms of torture to obtain a confession, the accused would naturally confess to anything. Torture made people confess to all the typical actions attributed to witchcraft: encounters with Satan, gathering on the witches' Sabbath, and using magic to harm others. Many of them hoped to stop the torture by giving away names of their neighbours.

Figure 12: Created in 1555, this one-leaf German print captures a poignant scene of the witch burnings that took place in Derenburg, Germany. The artwork portrays the act of witches being consumed by flames. Its serves as a haunting reminder of this dark chapter in history. Provided by R. Decker - Public domain, via Wikimedia Commons (https://commons.wikimedia.org/wiki/File:Zeitung_Derenburg_1555_crop.jpg)

France

In France, a woman with an important role in The Hundred Years' War and a leader of the French resistance against the English invaders was one woman that died by burning. That woman was Joan of Arc, a peasant who became a soldier. She fought to take Charles VII of France to the throne that was taken by the English king. Joan was accused of heresy because she claimed to be visited by angels and was acting under divine guidance.

After the defeat of her troops, she was taken prisoner by the English and accused of heresy. Reason given included her use of men's clothes on the battlefield, and having demoniac visions. Since Joan refused to confess and accept the church conditions, she was tried for witchcraft, found guilty, and condemned to die at the stake in 1431 at the age of 19. Later, an inquisitorial court revised the process of her trial and concluded that it had not been just. She was considered a martyr of the Catholic Church. Joan of Arc was later canonised in 1920, becoming one of the patron saints of France. Although her execution was due to political causes and not as a result of the witch craze, it is an example of how witchcraft as a crime could be deliberately used for different purposes.

Switzerland

Switzerland was heavily affected by the trials, and thousands of people were accused of witchcraft. The first recorded case of witchcraft in Switzerland dates back to 1427 in the canton of

Valais. The persecution of alleged witches increased in the 16th century, with the majority of cases taking place between 1560 and 1670. During this time, witch hunts were driven by religious and political tensions, with accusations of witchcraft being used as a means of social control. Accusations of witchcraft continued until the late 18th century.

The last witch trial recorded in Europe was that of Anna Göldi. She was a Swiss woman executed in 1782 in Glarus, Switzerland. Göldi worked as a maid for the Tschudi family. She was accused of putting needles in the milk of the Tschudi family's youngest child. Göldi was subsequently accused of being a witch and practicing witchcraft. She was arrested and put on trial, which lasted for several years. Despite her protestations of innocence, Göldi was found guilty and sentenced to death by decapitation. Her execution was carried out on June 13, 1782, making her the last person to be executed for witchcraft in Europe.

Göldi's case has since become a symbol of injustice and a reminder of the dangers of superstition and hysteria. It is said that the last words Anna spoke before her execution were: "I am innocent, yet I perish". Anna Göldi was posthumously pardoned in 2008—over two centuries after her death. In recent years, there have been attempts to rehabilitate Anna Göldi's memory, including a memorial plaque being dedicated to her in Switzerland.

Witchcraft and the Witch Trials in Italy

Italy has a long history of witch trials, with the majority taking place in the late 16th and early 17th centuries. In modern times, studies have been conducted to better understand the historical context of these witch trials and their lasting implications. While the purpose of this book is not to delve into all the particular regions, we shall briefly highlight the relevant differences that will allow us to understand the most remarkable cases in the territory of current Italy.

The Inquisition was responsible for many of these prosecutions, which occurred mostly in northern Italy. Before this, in the 14th century, Italy was, along with Flemish regions, the most dynamic area of Europe. The evolution of industries and the intense commerce activities were bringing more and more people to the city. The process of demographic and economic changes was faster than in other parts of the continent. It was followed by one of the most revolutionary shifts in thinking in history—the Renaissance. It was a cultural movement that encompassed an evolution in the way of thinking. It opened the doors to Modernity by retrieving the contributions of the classic Greeks and Romans to arts and science. It implied departing from the Catholic principles about life that placed God in the centre of the universe, and replacing that idea with a special concern for human beings, their beauty, and their ability to learn. This shift not only ushered in a new paradigm for understanding the relationship between humans and nature, progress, and life, but it also laid the groundwork for technological advancements and most importantly, rational thinking.

These changes were monumental both in societal structures and, more significantly, in people's mindsets. People posed a challenge to the traditional power structures. One consequence of this was the heightened intensity of the witch craze in Italy (Ben-Yehuda, 1980; Breslaw, 2000). Some of the earliest witch hunts and trials occurred in Italian villages. While these events have long been shrouded in mystery for many scholars and historians, evidence now indicates that they resulted in the death of hundreds of people.

Duni (2020) argues that studying witchcraft and witch hunts in Italy requires careful consideration. These arguments need to include the varied notions of witchcraft that existed during the transition from the Middle Ages to the early Modern period. This is particularly important because, during this time, Italy was not a unified state. It did not have centralised power, and different regions and communities held distinct beliefs related to witchcraft. Instead, it was a set of domains and principalities with their own legislation. This political and legal diversity created different approaches to witchcraft accusations. Therefore, the conditions for those considered witches and wizards were different in Northern Italy from those in the central regions or Southern Italy.

The conception of witchcraft is tied to folk practices that had been established for centuries in the peasant communities and were encompassed in diverse political and legal backgrounds. In the North and the Centre, witchcraft was associated with the term *strega* and its practitioners were "persecuted harshly, but only in some parts of Italy and for a relatively short time—at least as far as church courts, such as the Inquisition, were concerned" (Duni, 2020). In contrast, in the South, witchcraft was associated with the practice of *magiara* or *masciara*. The witches of *magiara* were believed to fly at night, have a pact with the Devil, and gather for the Sabbath. Those accused of *magiara* were "the object of sustained attention from tribunals throughout the entire period but were dealt with in fairly lenient terms, especially by the Inquisition" (Duni, 2020).

Although there were hundreds of prosecutions, executions less common (Duni, 2020). Northern Italy witnessed some of the earliest witch trials in Europe when the Renaissance was in splendour. Mass trials took place in cities like Milan, Cuneo, Pavia, Valtellina, and Canavese, among others, in the 14th and 15 centuries. The Italian wars—which was another condition for social unrest—that occurred in the first half of the 16th century were the peak of the witch craze. There was a second wave of trials in the 17th century that coincided with the Catholic Counter-Reformation process. Another scholarly research carried out by Dashu (2012) presents the collected evidence about the mass arrests that took place in Italy. Burning was performed in different parts of Italy between the end of the 15th century and at the beginning of the 17th century.

Figure 13: Showing the timeless representation of the fascination and fear associated with witchcraft during the Renaissance period. The Witches by Hans Baldung, 1508. Public domain, via Wikimedia Commons (https://commons.wikimedia.org/wiki/File:Baldung_Hexen_1508_kol.JPG)

One of the most tragic witch hunts in Italy occurred in the community of Triora, a village close to the border with France. A wave of witch-craze was triggered there and spread for years to nearby areas. In 1587, women of all social classes were accused of witchcraft, including poor peasants, and the daughters of the wealthiest landlords. About 30 women were prosecuted without relevant evidence. The testimonies and accusations against them were probably due to a famine that swept through the community. The women were imprisoned and tortured for years. In the end, none were condemned, as the trials never took place. However, many of them never survived their ordeals.

Another renowned case of the witch hunt in Italy took place in the Valcamonica valley (Tavuzzi, 2007). The population of the village included Albanian immigrants with rustic practices that aroused suspicions: "The sect was widely believed to hold regular, extremely populous sabbats on the Tonale mountains [...] (and) at least five thousand were deemed to be adepts of the sect of the witches" (Tavuzzi, 2007). Additionally, they were believed to spread their practices to the region of the Alps. Although it is uncertain how many people were prosecuted in the region, Tavuzzi's (2007) research points out that the Italian Inquisition prosecuted hundreds of people, many of them were sentenced to die at the stake, even though the judicial processes were riddled with irregularities. The evidence that has been collected exposed the cruelty of the procedure and the execution of mostly women who were burned alive.

In Italy, most of the accused and the condemned to death were women. According to Duni's research (2020), over 70% were women. Most of them were young women in fertile ages. According to the records, the accusers recognised no difference between spinsters, widows, and married women. Also, the accusations were not only directed at poor peasant women; many of them lived in cities and belonged to middle-class families. However, they were women considered outsiders due to personal traits or antisocial behaviours.

As the witch trials of Italy began to decline in the 18th century, a new era of enlightenment brought about more humane treatment for accused witches and those who practised magic. The legacy of witchcraft in Italy lives on today. Many people still practise folk magic and divination practices that are drawn from ancient beliefs. Witchcraft is no longer persecuted or punished; however, it still carries much stigma in certain parts of Italian society. Despite this negative perception, many Italian people believe that there is power in magic and that it can be used to benefit oneself and others.

Witch Trials in Spain

The Spanish Inquisition led to a mass of witch trials that took place in Spain during the 16th and 17th centuries. Spain and Portugal did not experience the same demographic and economic changes as the rest of the continent. The 15th century represented the unification of the kingdom by the Catholic king and queen, Fernando from Aragon and Elizabeth from Castile. They had expelled the Islamic empire that had ruled the peninsula for over eight centuries.

The process of political unification was complemented by imposing Catholicism as the official religion, and the persecution of Jews and Muslims that were considered heretics. The Spanish Inquisition had been created in the 13th century and the Moors had been the main target. In 1492, the Reconquista represented the recovery of Granada, a city in the south that was the last bastion of the Arabic resistance, and the final consolidation of the Spanish kingdom. The *Malleus*

Maleficarum was published in Spain while the Reconquista was in progress. From then on, the Inquisition strengthened the power of the new monarchs and was dedicated to also pursuing Jewish people. It was the beginning of the Jewish diaspora from Spain.

At this time in Spain, Judaism and Islam were considered heretic religions, as they deviated from the only true and original religion, Catholicism. Although the initial motive was to eradicate the unfaithful, witchcraft was also considered heresy. According to Knutsen's research (2002), there were around 6,000 trials in Spain explicitly carried out by the Inquisition. This was, in fact, just one of the three institutions with jurisdiction over witchcraft. The others being the ecclesiastical authorities and the secular courts.

The Spanish Inquisition has left the best records of how witch trials were carried out. Knutsen's (2002) research delivered similar results to those in Italy. Most of the accused were young women, and many of them confessed their condition as witches. Similar to other countries, the confessions included the practice of magic, the encounter with the Devil, and the surrender of their soul to Satan. Although there is less evidence as to the fate of the accused witches after the trials, Kuntsen concludes that when they were convicted, it implied death, and in exceptional cases by burning.

Other, more lenient punishments for lesser crimes were also handed out to the accused. The most common of these was banishment. These were often further compounded by other religious penalties. Another common penance was the *auto de fe*:

a "lavish ceremony paraded the convicts in their penitentiary garments before the expectant crowd. For each one, their crimes and punishment were read to the crowd" (Knutsen, 2002). The Inquisition used this means of public humiliation both to punish and teach people about the destiny of all those who would neglect Catholicism. Executions were also preceded by *autos de fe*. However, some of these ceremonies were too expensive for the church, especially considering the number of prisoners they had. Many of the crimes were not serious and represented a low threat to society.

The Church would sometimes forgive some of the accused after the *autos de fe*. This way, it reinforced its power, showing the capability to punish but also to show mercy. Like all the European judicial systems in the Middle Ages and early Modernity, the public execution of the condemned played an important role as exemplary punishment and social control. It gained particular importance in the political system where the governing authorities were consolidating their power.

The most famous Spanish trials and executions took place in the recently conquered Basque Kingdom of Navarre in the Pirinee region in the early 16th century. Furthermore, other massive hunts were carried out in Catalonia in the 17th century. According to Pújol's research, "4,000 women were tortured and killed after the nation's 1563 Witchcraft Act" in Catalonia (Hammer, 2022). This region became a centre of witch hunts for 300 years, possibly due to its location far away from the central power in Madrid, and with a population composed of a majority of illiterate people, subject to feudal lords and their minions. Several pieces of evidence from the trials revealed that although men were usually accused of witchcraft, the majority were women. The testimonies show that the accusation was based on an association of misfortune—newborn babies dying, natural disasters, and crop failure, among others—to acts of witchcraft.

According to evidence, many of the women were accused of witchcraft because of their knowledge and use of herbs as remedies. According to The Interpretation Centre of Witchcraft (Hammer 2022), there is,

> A hall filled with jars of dried roots, plants, and other natural remedies. 'The victims were always single women, and they came from the margins of society,' she (the guide) tells me (the researcher). Traditional healers were often accused of being in league with the devil (para. 8).

In Spain, courtroom transcripts prove how the accused were interrogated and tortured to obtain a confession. The law had established that torture could be applied for three days and if the accused did not confess, they should be considered innocent, but it was not always complied with. Some of the accusations were based only on the testimony of people who affirmed to have the extraordinary quality of seeing invisible signs on women who were witches. People of all classes, including priests, were imprisoned and tortured based on unsubstantiated claims made by those seeking to gain favour with authorities or get rid of perceived enemies.

Witch trials in Spain continued until the middle of the 18th century when the practice was finally abolished.

Great Britain - A Quick History Lesson

Britain, as an island separated from the continent, had a different development of social and economic evolution. It was under the rule of the Roman Empire for a short period, and therefore the influence of the Latin culture was less than on the continent. Then, the expeditions of the Germanic tribes were less varied than in the rest of Europe. The Anglo-Saxons, and later, the Vikings and the Normans were the races that melded with the native tribes of the British islands—the Bretons and the Celts.

In the 15th century, England was going through a process of consolidation of secular power. The War of the Roses resulted in the accession of the Tudor dynasty to the throne of England. The evolution of the political events that intended the consolidation of the state was merged with religious processes. This would lead to a conflict between the Catholic church, and England's own Reformation. The overlapping of politics, diplomacy, and religion had a strong impact on the conception of witchcraft.

King Henry VIII was responsible for the English Reformation. He broke the link with the Vatican as the centre of the Catholic church's power and created his own religion, Anglicanism. The reason for the rupture had been the king's request to the pope for permission to divorce his wife. He desired to enter into matrimony with a wife who could bear a male heir for the crown. Although the pope accepted his first request to divorce Catherine of Aragon, it was rejected when he tried to divorce his third wife.

England's history is marked by religious persecution, exemplified by the expulsion, execution, and mistreatment of Protestants during the reign of Henry VIII's daughter, Mary. She became infamously known as "Bloody Mary". She was the daughter of Catherine of Aragon, the Spanish Catholic princess. When Mary arrived on the throne, she reimposed the practice of Catholicism as the official religion of the kingdom. Protestant heretics were persecuted and executed at the stake. After Mary's death in 1558, the second in the line of succession was princess Elizabeth. She was Anne Boleyn's daughter (also accused of witchcraft). Elizabeth succeeded her half-sister as Queen of England, and during her reign, she worked to restore Anglicanism as the dominant religion in the country once again.

Witchcraft in Britain

Witchcraft in continental Europe differed from Britain due to the history of continental Europe, as discussed. The islands had a different settlement process and the cultural development also differs from the rest of Europe. One significant difference was the way witchcraft was perceived and understood. In continental Europe, witchcraft was often associated with heresy and devil worship. In contrast, in Britain, witchcraft was seen as a form of folk magic and was not necessarily associated with devil worship. While there were also witch hunts and trials in Britain, they were less frequent and less severe than those on the continent. The Anglican Church, which was the dominant religious institution in Britain, did not have the same level of power and influence as the Catholic Church had on the continent. This may have contributed to the difference in attitudes towards witchcraft.

Another factor that contributed to the difference in the perception was the social and economic conditions at the time. In Britain, while there were also economic and social challenges, they were not as severe as on the continent, and there was more social stability. This may have led to a less fearful attitude towards witchcraft and a greater emphasis on practical magic, such as healing and protection.

England

In England, witch hunts reached their peak during the 16th and 17th centuries. Hundreds of alleged witches were put on trial and executed for practising supposedly evil forms of magic.

Several scholars (Hunt, 2022; Breslaw, 2000) affirm that witchcraft and the witch craze did not acquire the dimensions of the phenomenon in the continent. Other sources inform that between 3,000 and 4,500 people for Scotland and 1,000 people for England, between 1566 and 1685, were killed for witchcraft (Gwynn, n.d.).

In England, trials were not conducted by an ecclesiastical authority, but rather by secular jurisdiction. There was not an institution similar to the Inquisition. Hunt (2022) explores witch hunts under Queen Elizabeth I, Henry VIII's daughter in the middle of the 16th century:

> Elizabeth's ascension to the English throne meant the relinquishment of the Catholic hold on England. As a result, there were many Catholic plots against her life. These conspirators were particularly drawn to the use of witchcraft against Elizabeth, as it was believed to be both effective and difficult to detect. The use of witchcraft against Elizabeth was therefore much feared, and all Catholics were suspect (p. 3).

In England, witchcraft was conceived as a secular crime from 1542 onwards. However, it was an act of heresy for the church; it was judged and condemned by the secular laws. Confessions were also desired, but the permission to inflict torture to obtain them was prohibited. The accused were also not deprived of all their rights. The importance of evidence was also more relevant in England than on the continent. Two witnesses were needed for an accusation to be considered. "Judgments were rendered by lay juries and trials became public exhibitions. If the accused were found guilty of this or any other capital offence, death would be by hanging." (Breslaw, 2000). Death was reserved for the more serious cases for example if a witch was convicted of murder.

The procedures of the trials were different in England because the perception of witchcraft was different. Witchcraft became a crime in 1542. At this time, harm "through the use of invocation, conjuration, or sorcery to find money, or to waste, consume, or destroy any person, or to provoke anyone to unlawful love" (Breslaw, 2000) indicated *maleficium*.

Figure 14: 1613 English pamphlet with the words "Witches apprehended, examined, and executed." The illustration portrays the sight of a witch being submerged in a river. Public domain via Wikimedia Commons (https://commons.wikimedia.org/wiki/File:Witches_apprehended...,_16 13_Wellcome_M0016701.jpg)

No book on the subject of the history of witchcraft in England could be complete without including the infamous exploits of Matthew Hopkins. Commonly known as the Witchfinder General, Hopkins remains one of the most infamous figures in British history due to his merciless witch-hunting.

Matthew Hopkins was born in Suffolk, England, around 1620. Not much is known about his early life or upbringing. However, it is widely believed that he was the son of a Puritan clergyman. In 1644, at the height of the English Civil War, Hopkins and his associate John Stearne began their careers as witch-hunters. This was at a time when the country was embroiled in a power struggle between the Royalists and the Parliamentarians. It provided fertile ground for witch-hunting and Hopkins capitalised on this.

Hopkins claimed to have been appointed by Parliament, though there is no actual evidence of this. Regardless, he maintained that this supposed authority allowed him to travel across East Anglia, charging towns for his service in identifying and prosecuting alleged witches.

Hopkins and his associates used various brutal and inhumane methods to identify and convict those accused of witchcraft. One such method was "swimming" (Chapter 6) where the accused would be securely tethered and cast into a body of water. Hopkins also relied heavily on confessions extracted through sleep deprivation and other forms of torture. Accused witches were often kept awake for days on end until they confessed to their supposed crimes. He would then ask leading questions, which often resulted in false confessions. Between 1645 and 1647, Hopkins and Stearne were responsible for the persecution and execution of hundreds of alleged witches, making them the most prolific witch-hunters in English history. The vast majority of those accused were women, often elderly and vulnerable, who were unable to defend themselves against the charges. The most notorious of these trials was the Bury St. Edmunds witch trial in 1645, where 18 people were executed in a single day.

One of the most notorious techniques involved "witch pricking" where Hopkins would search the body of the accused for marks or blemishes that were believed to be the "Devil's mark." Hopkins and his associates believed that witches would have these secret marks, where their familiar would suckle. If a mark was found, it was considered proof of guilt. These marks, often just moles or birthmarks, were then pricked with needles. If the person felt no pain or the mark did not bleed, they were deemed guilty.

Hopkins' reign of terror was relatively short-lived. Criticism of his methods began to grow, and his support from local authorities waned. In 1647, he retired from his role as the Witchfinder General, and within a year, he passed away. The witch-hunting craze he had helped to fuel began to subside.

Figure 15: "The Examination of a Witch", by T. H. Matteson (1853). The work shows the court looking for a "witch mark". This captivating artwork is housed in the Peabody Essex Museum in Salem. T. H. Matteson. Public domain, via Wikimedia Commons (https://commons.wikimedia.org/wiki/File:Examination_of_a_Witch_-_Tompkins_Matteson.jpg)

Scotland

Scotland was different again. It had a far more severe attitude toward witches than England—very similar to the procedures in continental Europe. While in England, witches were not burned—although heretics were—accusations and executions by death on the stake were more common in Scotland (Gunn, 2003). As in England, the accusations of witchcraft in Scotland had a political connection.

An interesting example of this is the history of King James VI and his wife, Princess Ann of Denmark. Their rule was heavily scrutinised by the people. They questioned their authority to govern. There were widespread beliefs that the couple were being targeted by conspirators who were using witchcraft to undermine their rule. During the king and his wife's return to Scotland from Denmark, their ship encountered a fierce storm that nearly caused it to sink. The monarchs, in their search for an explanation, accused three maidservants of making a pact with the Devil to cause the king and queen's demise at sea. The women were subjected to torture, and eventually, they confessed to their alleged crimes. One of these maidservants was Agnes Sampson, previously mentioned in chapter 2.

Wales

Unlike what happened in England and Scotland, there were only a few witch trials in Wales. The cases of witchcraft here were isolated. They did not cause any of the subsequent witch hunt frenzies that occurred in England or Europe. Where witchcraft was suspected in Wales, it was mostly dealt with by their existing legal framework. According to several scholars (Gwynn, n.d.; Starling, 2022), magic is part of the cultural background in Wales, with a rooted tradition in their Celtic origins. The idea of witchcraft associated with *maleficium* never truly impacted Wales. Magical beliefs and rituals were part of the popular traditions, and magic was close to what we have defined as folk magic. This was mostly related to the knowledge of spells and the use of herbs to heal and help people. There are many words to refer to practitioners of magic: *Dewin, Consuriwr, Dyn Hysbys, Gwiddan, Rheibies, Swyngyfareddwyr, Planedydd, Daroganwr* (Starling, 2022), and none of them is equivalent to witch or sorcerer.

According to Starling (2022), the witch hysteria that had spread across the European continent and had reached England did not resonate in Wales:

> At a time when our neighbours the English were persecuting numerous innocent people under the guise of dealing with "Witches," the Welsh did not succumb to the hysteria. Witch trials did happen in Wales, but very rarely and usually in areas that were highly anglicized or influenced by England in some way (para. 15).

This research indicates that in Wales there were only five people accused of witchcraft who were executed in two centuries of their history.

There were less than 40 trials for witchcraft in Wales and they were considered under two types of accusation: witchcraft as slander and as *maleficium* (Twigg, 2021). All the accusations were against women. The main reasons given were infringements in social harmony. This means that women who had problems with their neighbours were more likely to be accused of witchcraft. According to Twigg's (2021) research, there were common themes which often determined the outcome of a trial. These could be physical appearance and personal traits. Or women who did not fit conventional female roles. These were all common reasons why a woman could be considered a witch. When there was social unrest or local conflicts involving witchcraft, other solutions were found. This was often in the form the payment of *galanas*. This was a Welsh law that involved payment made to the victim, or the family of the victim, by the person who had committed the crime against them.

Ireland

Witchcraft in Ireland has been shaped, not only the country's unique cultural and religious traditions, but also its tumultuous political and social history. From the early days of pagan Ireland to its Christianisation and the colonial period, the practice of witchcraft has played a significant role in the country's folklore and mythology. It has had a similar impact on its legal and religious institutions.

The pre-Christian era in Ireland was marked by the prevalent belief in the supernatural and the existence of various gods and goddesses. Some of these deities were associated with magic. An example was the goddess Brigid, who was revered as a patron of healing, of poetry, and of divination. Other pagan practices, such as the use of herbs, charms, and incantations, were also often used for healing or protection.

With the arrival of Christianity in the 5th century, the concepts of these practices shifted. In people's minds, these practices became increasingly associated with the Devil and considered a sin. The church's influence on Irish society led to the suppression of many pagan beliefs and practices, including what was believed to be witchcraft. As previously discussed, the first recorded case of witchcraft in Ireland occurred in 1324, when Alice Kyteler, a wealthy merchant, was accused of practicing witchcraft and heresy.

The 16th and 17th centuries saw a resurgence of witchcraft trials in Ireland, as the country was caught up in the wider European witch craze. Accusations of witchcraft in Ireland were often used as a way of settling personal scores or gaining advantage in local disputes. One of the most infamous cases was that of Florence Newton, a woman accused of bewitching a young girl in Youghal, County Cork, in 1661. Newton was arrested, tried, and eventually hanged. This marked the last recorded execution for witchcraft in Ireland.

During the colonial period, witchcraft continued to be a source of fear and suspicion in Irish society. The English authorities were particularly concerned about the practice of witchcraft among the population, seeing it as a threat to their political and religious authority. In 1711, the Irish Parliament passed the Witchcraft Act, which made it a crime to claim to have magical powers, or to accuse others of witchcraft. The act remained in force until 1821. There were no recorded cases of prosecutions under the law.

In the 20th century, the practice of witchcraft in Ireland underwent a revival, as part of a wider interest in neo-paganism and the occult. The formation of the Witchcraft Society of Ireland in the 1970s marked a turning point in the acceptance of witchcraft as a legitimate religious practice.

Chapter 8: The Witch Trials in North America

In this chapter, we will examine witchcraft in North America, specifically focusing on the American British colonies. From the infamous Salem witch trials to the broader cultural beliefs and practices surrounding witchcraft.

The subject of witchcraft played a significant role in the colonies' development and social dynamics. We will explore its origins and the role that religion and politics played.

The Impact of European Settlers in North America

The first British settlements in North America began at the beginning of the 17th century. These settlers were mostly people coming from England and establishing themselves on the Eastern Coast of the continent. Later, groups of colonists from Germany and the Netherlands settled in these new territories. Most of the new settlers from England were puritans. They were parishioners of the Church of England and professed Anglicanism, the religious order established by Henry VIII. The puritans considered that their church had preserved the core principles of Christianity. They settled in the new cities of Massachusetts Bay Colony, Saybrook, Connecticut, Rhode Island, and New Hampshire. Another religious community that settled in the colonies were the Quakers. This was a "Christian group that arose in mid-17th-century England, dedicated to living under the 'Inner Light,' or direct inward apprehension of

God, without creeds, clergy, or other ecclesiastical forms" (Vann, 2022). Some of the colonies were declared a safe refuge for Roman Catholics. These new colonies proved to be a secure place for them to live and practice their faith.

As discussed in chapter 5, the colonists arrived in the Atlantic World, bringing with them the European ideas of witchcraft, and in particular, that of perceived heresy. Many Europeans at this time regarded other religions with scepticism. Indeed, some others, with more extreme views, considered practitioners of different religious faiths were followers of the Devil. English colonisers first intended to convert the native American populations to their faith. In many cases, this did not work.

The African population brought to the colonies a few years later, started at a time when the foundation of the cities were being built. These people were enslaved on the African coasts and brought into the colonies. According to Breslaw, the British tolerated, or even ignored the African rituals. In the long term, the African enslaved people had a low cultural exchange with the colonialists. This was due to their enforced lower position in society: "the result was the retention of many shared African ideas about the spiritual realm and the imaginative merging of magical practices taken from a variety of cultures" (Breslaw, 2000).

The British migration to the American lands had strong political and religious motivations. They were searching to settle where they could have more freedom to express their private and individual rights. This led to an early development of self-government, and each colony was established as an independent city. Even though they had a common cultural background that included legislation and religious beliefs, each community had its own jurisdiction and particularities. Since most of them were based on religious communities, the colonies were societies with high levels of moral standards, and parishes played a central role in the organisation. Although they had church and state as separate institutions, the strong moral principles influenced by Puritanism and Quakerism were the basis for the social order.

The British colonies in America have their own chapter in history regarding witch hunts and trials. The native communities that were considered to be associated with the Devil due to their practices had been displaced and obliged to move to the West. However, accusations of witchcraft appeared within the communities. At the end of the 17th century, while in Europe the witch craze began to diminish, the witchcraft hysteria moved to the New World.

Massachusetts was one of the original colonies of the first British immigrants. They were Puritan refugees escaping from England. The Puritans established a theocratic government—a secular government but with legislation totally aligned with religious principles. Limited to church members, it prevented any independence of other religious views.

With this scene set, we now look at one of the most renowned witch trials in history: The Salem trials.

Massachusetts: The Salem Trials

The Salem witch trials are one of the most well-known examples of mass hysteria, religious extremism, and false accusations that have been recorded in American history. The trials took place in colonial Massachusetts between February 1692 and May 1693. The trials resulted in the executions of 20 people, mostly women, accused of practising witchcraft or being involved in a conspiracy against the Puritan-led government. Hundreds of other people were also accused but ultimately released after lengthy interrogations and examinations.

At that time, the laws against witchcraft were the same as in England. The Witchcraft Act of 1604, *An Act against Conjuration, Witchcraft, and Dealing with Evil and Wicked Spirits,* was in full force. According to the Act, practices of witchcraft were considered a felony, and the accused received a minor penance if found guilty. However, if people were accused and condemned for witchcraft twice, the punishment was death. In fact, Witchcraft, as a crime, was one of the twelve capital offences that were included in the first statute of the law of the colony, *The Book of the General Lawes and Libertyes Concerning the Inhabitants of Massachusetts*, printed in 1648 (Smith, 2017).

In the late 17th century, the English monarchy started a colonial war with France that significantly disrupted everyday life. The conflict led to significant demographic shifts as populations were forcibly relocated. People coming from the affected areas moved into other cities, Salem village (now Danvers), among them. This internal migration placed "a strain on Salem's resources, aggravating the existing rivalry between families with ties to the wealth of the port of Salem and those who still depended on agriculture. (…) The Puritan villagers believed all the quarrelling was the work of the devil" (Blumberg, 2022).

The witch hunt in Salem was triggered by a series of events that unfolded amidst mounting social tensions. It is believed that it began with two young girls, aged 9 and 12, one of whom was a minister's daughter. The girls suddenly began experiencing fits that defied medical explanation. Their symptoms included screaming, contorting their bodies into unusual positions, and speaking an incomprehensible language. After a group of Puritans consulted another local minister for advice, they began to investigate who or what might be responsible. The townspeople believed that the girls were under the influence of witchcraft.

The girls accused three women of having used magic to hurt them: Tituba, an enslaved woman that worked for the minister's family, a homeless woman named Sarah Good, and Sarah Osborne, an older poor woman. They were taken to trial and although two of the women claimed they were innocent; Tituba confessed to witchcraft. Tituba, was a slave from the Caribbean who was brought to Salem by her owners. At the beginning of the trial, Tituba denied anything related to occultism or supernatural evil forces, but then she surrendered and rendered a confession alleging her participation in rituals, "service to the devil, riding on sticks, and being told by a black dog to harm the children" (Polkes et al., 2019) and also that she had signed the book of the Devil. After her initial confession, Tituba recanted her statement, claiming that it resulted from harsh interrogation techniques that had made her confess. Despite escaping execution, Tituba spent 13 long months in prison, and her owner abandoned her.

Amidst a frenzy of mass hysteria, numerous people became caught up in a wave of extraordinary events, which were often attributed to supposed witches. Testimonies arose everywhere, and anyone could be a witch. Over 200 people were prosecuted in Salem for witchcraft crimes, and 20 of them were condemned to death by hanging. The trials would admit testimonies of visions and dreams, and spectral evidence to declare a person guilty. In 1693, the Superior Court of Massachusetts interfered and prohibited these as proof of crimes. The main victims of the Salem trials were primarily women, particularly those who were poor, marginalised, and had little social or economic power. More specifically, it is believed that around 78% of those accused were women, and 52% were unmarried. Many of the accused were from the lower socio-economic classes of the time, including farmers, labourers, and servants. Other victims included women who were socially isolated, such as widows or those who had no family or community ties.

Accusations of witchcraft in Salem often came from individuals who had a personal vendetta against the accused, such as neighbours or family members. This led to false accusations and a climate of fear and suspicion which contributed to the hysteria and persecution of innocent people. The trials exposed the dangers of religious fanaticism, intolerance, and the misuse of power in the name of justice.

Figure 16: This oil on canvas work captures the haunting scene of two individuals accused of witchcraft standing trial in Salem, Massachusetts during the notorious witch hunts that took place there. Howard Pyle, Public domain, via Wikimedia Commons (https://commons.wikimedia.org/wiki/File:There_is_a_flock_of_yellow_birds_around_her_head.jpg)

Some of the victims of the Salem witch trials include:

Bridget Bishop: Bishop was the first person to be tried and executed during the Salem witch trials. She was accused of bewitching several girls, and her reputation as a tavern owner and independent woman made her an easy target.

Rebecca Nurse: Rebecca Nurse was a seventy-one-year-old widow living in Salem Village, Massachusetts at the time of the trials. Nurse was a respected member of the community and a devout Christian. However, she was accused of witchcraft by her neighbours, who believed that her piety was a mask for her supposed malevolent powers. Despite her family's efforts to clear her name, she was convicted and hanged on July 19th, 1692.

Giles Corey: Corey was one of the first people accused by the Salem villagers of practising witchcraft. He was also among those who were arrested and put on trial for sorcery. During his trial, he refused to enter either a plea of guilt or innocence because he believed that doing so would be tantamount to admitting that the court had authority over him. As punishment for his refusal, magistrates decided to subject him to pressing, a form of torture in which heavy stones were placed on his body until he eventually died.

Martha Corey: Martha was the wife of Giles Corey and was accused of witchcraft along with her husband. She was convicted and hanged despite her protestations of innocence.

John Proctor: Proctor was a farmer and tavern owner who was well-respected in the community. However, he was accused of witchcraft by his former servant, Abigail Williams. His wife, Elizabeth Proctor, was also accused. John Proctor was hanged. His legacy has endured through Arthur Miller's play, "The Crucible".

Daniel Spofford: In the winter of 1692, Daniel Spofford was accused of witchcraft in Salem. He pleaded not guilty to all charges but was still found guilty by a jury of his peers. He escaped execution as Governor William Phips granted him a reprieve on June 17th, 1693 due to doubts about his guilt. Though he was spared death, Daniel Spofford still suffered due to the accusations against him. He lost both his home and livelihood as a result of being targeted, forcing him to leave Salem.

The hunt quickly spread beyond Salem Village with more people being accused of being witches by their neighbours or family members. Despite the lack of solid evidence, many people were convicted based on hearsay and circumstantial evidence. Those accused had no legal rights to due process and were often subjected to lengthy interrogations and examinations to extract confessions. Many confessed to save themselves from execution despite not actually having committed any crimes. In May 1693, the Massachusetts General Court declared that the accusations against those accused of witchcraft had been unfounded and reversed all convictions related to the witch hunts.

Some scholars have suggested that the consumption of contaminated grain may have led to symptoms that were interpreted as being caused by witchcraft. In particular, grain may have been infected with a fungus called Claviceps purpurea (also known as Ergot fungus). This is known to cause hallucinations and other symptoms similar to those described. It is worth noting that this theory is not universally accepted.

Maryland

This colony was settled to provide Roman Catholics a safe place to escape from the religious restrictions of Protestant England and to practise their faith freely. The Calverts were the foundational members of the colony. They established religious freedom within the bounds of Trinitarian Christianity. Later, the founders converted to Protestantism, but the colony continued to receive parishioners of other religious groups.

There are many records of witch hunts and trials in Maryland, some of which resulted in the execution of the accused. These executions were not carried out in the colony's territory but on the ship, Charity. One of the first witch trials was against a woman named Mary Lee, accused of having "summoned a relentless storm by the malevolence of the witches" (Quesenbery, 2013). She was tried, condemned, and executed without further evidence.

There is another famous witch trial in Maryland that involved an English immigrant, Rebecca Fowler. One of Rebecca's male servants reported to the authorities that Rebecca had cast a spell to curse him. In 1685, she was arrested and put on trial. The court accused her of witchcraft and found her guilty of causing the servants illness. Again, the only evidence found against her was the testimony of the same man that was accusing her. Shortly after the trial began, Rebecca was executed by hanging.

Perhaps the most famous witchcraft case in Maryland that was taken as a popular legend and made into a film. The story of Moll Dyer is told in The Blair Witch Project. There is no official record of this case, and it was more about superstition than a judicial trial. Dyer was accused of witchcraft by her neighbours and a group of men chased her through the woods on a winter's night. She tried to escape, but later, she was found dead, frozen. Then, hundreds of stories of the woman being a witch, and haunting the place around where she was found arose.

These cases of witchcraft in Maryland all occurred at the end of the 17th century, and some patterns are repeated: the accused are women, no evidence was found to prove even the practice of witchcraft, and all the accusations came from social hysteria.

Pennsylvania

The way that witchcraft accusations were solved in Pennsylvania differed totally from the rest of the colonies and most of the cases that have been described. There was a single case of a witchcraft trial, and how it was conducted by the established authority. However, William Penn, the founder of Pennsylvania, prevented any hysteria from spreading to the community.

Two Swedish immigrant women were accused by their own neighbours of having killed their livestock by means of witchcraft. The women were taken to the trial led by Penn. Since one woman did not speak English, Penn provided not only her with an interpreter but also included Swedish people as witnesses. Further, he allowed the accused to defend themselves in the trial. This was innovative, not only in the colonies, but for the English legal system in general, since women lacked the right to testify in court. The trial was no different from others: people testified about having witnessed witchcraft practices. However, in this case, the judge did not consider these testimonies as evidence. The women were found guilty of Witchcraft, but not of the crimes they were accused of. They were condemned to pay a fee. The distinctive pattern here was that the judge made it a public trial and demonstrated to the community some testimonies could not be proven. This undoubtedly helped prevent hysteria which would have provoked further witch hunts.

Chapter 9: The History of Witchcraft in Russia

The practice of witchcraft in Russia has been shaped by a variety of cultural and historical influences. In this chapter, we will explore its history of witchcraft, including its origins, and the role that religion, politics, and cultural beliefs played.

Just like Europe and the Americas, it is important to understand the history of Russia and its beginnings to better understand its own unique aspects of witchcraft.

Russia - A Quick History Lesson

The economic, social, and political evolution of Russia is rather different from the rest of Europe. Russia is the largest country in the world, and it has its territories spread over two continents; Asia and Europe. The Asian side of the country beyond the Ural Mountains is represented by the steppes and tundra of Siberia. This has always had a low population density due to the extreme climate conditions. On the other side, the territories concentrate most of the population in the principal cities. Being such a big country, it has a heterogenous ethnical and cultural composition.

The predecessors of this vast country were the Slav tribes of central Europe, which spread and occupied the lands toward the East and merged with other local groups of people. When the

Western Roman Empire collapsed after the fall of Byzantium under the Turks, the Slav populations received the influence of the Greek Catholics. Byzantine missionaries, Cyrillus and Methodius, developed a spoken language to evangelise the Slavs and developed the Cyrillic script to translate the Bible.

The Vikings—Varangians to the Byzantines—and their cultural heritage of the Scandinavian people entered the continent, navigating the rivers from the Baltic region. They merged with the Slavs and founded the first state called the Kievan Rus' in the 10th century. First, the king converted to Christianism, and then, in a public, massive baptism, the whole population also became Christian. Over time, the practice of Slavic paganism was gradually supplanted by Christianity. However, many elements of the pagan tradition were absorbed into Christian practices, and some continue to be observed in various forms to this day.

These territories also received the invasion and social influence of other cultural groups, like the Mongolians and the Tartars. In the 12th century, while Europe was going through the late Middle Ages, Moscow, and what would later become the Russian empire, were founded. The predominant ethnicity were the Slavs.

Witchcraft in Russia

The history of witchcraft in Russia dates back to the pre-Christian era, when it was seen as a form of nature worship. Throughout this time and into the mediaeval period, witches were believed to be able to use their supernatural powers to harm others or bring good luck. Witches were persecuted during this time in Russia, particularly by the Russian Orthodox Church and early Tsars.

Magical practices were common in Slavic Russia and mostly consisted of pre-Christian spells and rituals. One of the most relevant practices of the Slav communities was *zagovory*. This is an "East Slavic folk tradition, in which magical practitioners called *znakhari* (literally, those who know) practice magical healing incantations" (Shukla, 2021). Zagovory consists of oral compositions that have been used over generations as part of their ancestral heritage. They are presented in a formulaic language and provide people with explanations of the world that surrounds them. Besides the language, they have special receptacles to prepare mixtures of herbs for use in Zagovory rituals. According to Shukla (2021), the term zagovory can be translated into English as "charms" or "spells", but not as witchcraft, particularly in its association with maleficium. The objectives of zagorovy were various. It could be used for alleviating pain, fighting misfortune, and protecting from harm.

Zagovory can be compared to the practices of the cunning folk described in continental Europe. In the same way, zagovory practitioners were called *znakhar*, which also means sorcerer/sorceress, healer, or witch doctor (Shukla, 2021). The practice of zagorovy was condemned by the East Orthodox church and its ecclesiastical authorities. However, the practitioners of znakhar continued to exist. In a society with no trained physicians and late scientific development, zagorovy remained the only option that people had to treat their illnesses. These practices continued to exist after the unification of the tribes under the tsar's power. In fact, the practices were widespread and "Everyone from the tzar's wife to the lowliest serf might turn to magic at some juncture in their lives." (Kivelson, 2022).

Besides the practice of zagorovy, magical practices were common among the rural communities in Russia and the Ukraine. Most of them consisted of the use of herbs, the production of potions and charms, and the chanting of spells. These were created both by magic specialists and ordinary people. The Slav people also believed that anyone could communicate with spirits and deities and control supernatural forces to make things happen. They used these magical practices to heal, for divination, and for influencing others. Some of them used magic for malevolent objectives and believed that they could be used for bewitchment.

The most common spells were of two types; Love spells and "spells of power". Slavic witchcraft has a rich tradition of love spells. These were used to attract or enhance romantic relationships. These spells involved the use of herbs (particularly those with aphrodisiac properties), crystals (rose quartz or garnet), candles, and other objects. Herbs used could include yarrow, damiana, or rose petals, among others. The herbs were typically combined in a sachet or charm bag, and would be carried or worn by the person seeking to attract a lover. The use of candles, which are often used to represent the energy of love and passion, would be carved with symbols or words. The candles would be burned during a ritual, with the intention of attracting love.

The "spells of power", were used by people to "counteract a rigid hierarchical system". These spells were a way to protect themselves from injustice and arbitrariness. According to Kivelson (2022),

> While women were often stuck at home or on estates, men of all ranks, even serfs, were relatively mobile. During their outings, they might run up against the arbitrary authority of a master, a judge, an official, a military officer, a nobleman, or a bishop (para. 18).

Dvoeverie

The most important system of beliefs, myths, and practices of the Slavish people between the 8th to 13th centuries was paganism or *dvoeverie*. Dvoeverie is a concept that refers to the coexistence of two different belief systems, typically used in the context of Russian culture. Specifically, it is used to describe the phenomenon of pagan beliefs and practices coexisting alongside Christianity within a given community or individual.

Most scholars believe that dvoeverie emerged as a result of the Christianisation of pagan communities in Russia. As Christianity spread across the region, it encountered pre-existing pagan beliefs and practices. These beliefs were continued alongside Christian rituals and traditions. The term dvoeverie itself suggests a sense of ambiguity or ambivalence in these practices. On the one hand, individuals and communities profess adherence to Christianity and participate in Christian rituals and practices. On the other hand, they also continue to observe pre-Christian beliefs and practices, such as the veneration of nature spirits or the use of magical charms and rituals.

The name of "paganism" to this system of beliefs was given by outsiders—travellers and historians—but for the Slav people, it was simply part of their religion (Meet the Slavs, 2021). Many symbols and rituals were overridden by the process of Christianisation by the end of the 12th century. This was a slow process. In many regions, it did not penetrate the traditional structures of rural communities deeply. Dvoeverie has been a topic of interest and debate among scholars of Russian history and culture. Some argue that it represents a form of resistance to Christianisation, and a means of preserving traditional beliefs and practices. Others suggest that it is a form of syncretism, or the blending of different religious traditions.

Witchcraft Practices

Among the pagans, there remains the figurehead of old believers. These were practitioners of sorcery believed to possess supernatural powers to conjure spells and carry out magical rituals. Their mission was to help people to better understand natural phenomena and protect them from misfortune. They played a social role as intermediaries with the deities, offering to guarantee peace and a good harvest. They carried out magical rituals that combined natural elements and specific words, or spells.

For the ancient Slavs, the origins of witchcraft are rather different from western European people. In Slavic mythology, witches are considered to be terrifying demons or vampires who took the shape of women to attack human beings. They also have the myth of "the first witch" which is a legend that has been transmitted generation after generation:

The story relates that a woman was caught in the rain whilst she was collecting food in the woods. She took off her clothes and kept them in a bag to keep them dry. When the rain stopped, the woman dressed up again with her clothes perfectly dry. Then, the horned god Veles—a Slavic pagan god—appeared to the woman and asked her to explain how she had avoided getting her clothes wet. She agreed, but only on the condition that Veles would impart his magic in return. The god did. But the woman then lied to him. Instead of telling him the simple explanation about the bag, she invented a story. The god found out he had been deceived and transformed the woman into the first witch, readily invested with all of the god's magical powers.

The Slavs believed that most, if not all witches, were women. Specifically, women who had died and had received the wrong funeral ritual, or none at all. They would return from death and be transformed into witches, sometimes adopting the shape of animals like cats or ravens. Witches were associated with evil and were particularly feared in the Spring and the White Night

Feast—moments of the year when witches were believed to visit their lands.

In Slavic Russia, witchcraft was seen as a powerful force. The traditional belief among the Russian people was that witches had access to magical powers, which could be used for both good and bad. Witches were often feared and respected by the general population because of their ability to influence events and control nature with their spells. Though much of the traditional witchcraft practised in Slavic Russia is now considered obsolete, it still holds an important place in the history and culture of the country. Its influence can be seen in many aspects of modern Russian life, from superstitions to traditional beliefs. Even today, many people believe that witches have a real power to affect their lives and destinies, making them an ever-present part of Russian folklore.

The Kupala Festival

One of the most important rituals in Slavic paganism was the Kupala festival, named after the Slavic god of fertility. The Kupala festival, which was celebrated (and still is) in midsummer, is a traditional Slavic holiday that celebrates the summer solstice, which falls on June 21st. It is associated with fertility and the harvest. During this festival, people gather around bonfires and engage in various rituals, including jumping over fire and weaving wreaths of flowers.

Over time, the Kupala Festival was influenced by Christianity and the celebration of the Christian saint, John the Baptist.

However, it still retains many elements of pagan traditions and beliefs. Today, it is celebrated in many Slavic countries, including Russia, Ukraine, Belarus, and Poland.

The Witch Trials in Russia

Witch trials increased late in the 16th century, culminating in Ivan IV's "Great Witch Hunt" of 1571-1572. During this period, hundreds of people were accused and subsequently executed. By this time, witchcraft in Russia was thought to be a causing factor behind catastrophes such as famine, plagues, and diseases (Zguta, 1977). The context was characterised by the distressing reign of Ivan the Terrible and the Time of Troubles, with high levels of social unrest due to foreign invasions and famine. The political landscape of the time also had a significant impact on the tsar's ability to maintain power. Particularly as a new dynasty, the Romanovs attempted to ascend to the throne. Finally, a religious crisis provoked by the great schism of the official church, contributed to a further increment in the witch craze. However, it did not achieve the same levels as in western Europe.

By the 17th century, many Russians had adopted a belief system based on paganism and nature worship. It incorporated elements akin to witchcraft. This revival included the use of charms, spells and magical objects to invoke supernatural powers. Witchcraft was seen as a way to gain power or influence in all areas of life, from health and fertility to trade and politics. Many superstitions arose about witches, such as believing that they could fly on broomsticks or transform into animals. This fear gave rise to various rituals and symbols associated with witchcraft in Russia, such as the use of herbal mixtures and talismans for protection against evil forces.

Although Catholicism was the official religion in Slavic Russia, their perspective of witchcraft differed from the hegemonic conception of Catholics and Protestants in Europe. As the Slavic people had received the influence of the Byzantine empire, they tended to assume similar concepts and practices passed to them from this source. They didn't include ideas about the witches' Sabbaths or the satanic origins of witchcraft. According to investigations by Litinas Markos (2016), Orthodox traditions ruled over varied ethnic groups. Litinas analysed three differences with the West:

- a theological difference in the concept of the Devil and its powers, and the nature and use of magic;
- legal treatment of witchcraft that had different punishments;
- and the influence of Islam on the religious nuances.

But also, on people's behaviours at that time, who "were more susceptible to incorporating unorthodox superstitions and practices into their belief systems."

For the Orthodox church, any practice of magic was evil even if the result was harmless. Unlike the West, the Eastern Orthodox church did not emphasise women more likely to practice witchcraft. Litinas (2016) states that,

Both male and female words are used to describe culprits of magic, although in most cases, the word "heretic" is preferred. Also, there is no extensive chapter explaining why women are more vulnerable to magic, as in *Malleus*. Orthodox theology believed that men and women could equally be tricked into committing the sin of magic (p. 24).

According to Kivelson's (2022) research, around 75% of the accused of witchcraft in Russia were men. One reason for this was that there was no direct or assumed connection between women and the Devil. The author affirms that although women were subordinated to men, there were other hierarchical differences that played a major role. It was a strong hierarchically shaped society where the most important differences were determined by status and age. Although women were at a lower stage in the social pyramid, men without status were more likely to be persecuted for witchcraft. Most of the accused were itinerants, homeless, wanderers, and also "foreigners".

Although the existence of witches was related to evil, they were not considered a threat to the church. The goal of the church was aimed at rehabilitation, rather than elimination. In the East, there was a predominant idea of the Devil as less powerful than God. Therefore, wizards and witches were not seen as people involved in rituals invoking the Devil, but were perceived as the victims of illusions. It was less important if they were practicing magic or not. In the West, having the conviction of being a witch was used as evidence to condemn; in the East, they were less likely to believe that they could harm. The Orthodox Church in Russia does not have an equivalent to the Malleus Maleficarum or to the Inquisition. There were no special institutions that were in charge of inquiries and prosecution for witchcraft. It was not considered a secular crime either. *Against the Types of Magic* is a demonological document written in the 19th century, much later than the witch craze that took place in Western Europe. It was a rare contribution to Orthodox theology and endeavoured to establish the general guidelines to judge witchcraft.

In Russia, like in many other regions of Europe but in different ways, religion played an important role in the state's consolidation. Therefore, there is a slight border between secular and religious power. In 1551, the Orthodox Church condemned witchcraft and asked Tsar Ivan to implement the death penalty to eradicate it from the rural population. The church was trying to impose Christianism, and for that, it had to confront paganism, witchcraft practitioners, sorcerers, and astrologers. The prosecution was carried out by the ecclesiastical authorities, and the sentence and execution were perpetrated by secular courts. First, the tsar did not introduce the death penalty, but it was eventually implemented in 1653. Those accused and condemned for all types of paganism as sorcery received the penalty of death by burning.

Kivelson and Worobec (Cornell University Press, n.d.) carried out research about witchcraft in Russia and the Ukraine and collected evidence of several witch trials that took place in the region. According to their sources, the trials included a case of a Siberian trapper found in possession of a book of spells. It was alleged that he used these spells to further his success in trap setting, as well as attracting and bewitching women. Also, the case of an Orthodox priest who cast spells to earn the goodwill of his masters. A further case is recorded of a military man who assisted the emperor to fight and defeat the Prussian kingdom by using witchcraft techniques.

There were earlier cases of witch trials in the 11th century when people were executed for their use of witchcraft in relation to a food shortage (Zguta, 1977). This was also a frequent reason for witchcraft accusations during the 13th century when there was a severe famine. Those blamed for witchcraft were judged and executed by burning or by cold water. Later, in the 17th century, there were only just over 90 people brought to trial for witchcraft in all the territories of the empire.

Trials in this region diverged from those in Western Europe in several ways. While interrogations and torture to extract confessions were still prevalent, spectral evidence—testimonies of supernatural occurrences—typically did not hold as much weight in determining the fate of the accused. Instead, physical evidence discovered within the accused's home or possessions often sufficed for a guilty verdict. Such evidence could comprise herbs, potions, and written spells.

During the early half of the 18th century, witch trials still persisted. However, a significant shift occurred in the criminal perception of witchcraft. The majority of the accused were soldiers, clergymen, and individuals affiliated with the tsar's court. This is also one of the primary reasons why the number of men accused and convicted of witchcraft exceeded that of women during this period. This highlights the distinct difference of the witch trials in this region compared to Western Europe.

As the decade's past, witch trials continued to take place, but were now much less common than they had been in previous centuries. There was a growing acceptance that witches could be beneficial rather than criminal. Particularly when it came to healing sickness or predicting future events. During this time, occultism became increasingly popular among members of Russia's upper classes who saw it as a fashionable pursuit. The 19th century saw an increased focus on superstition and the occult, including witchcraft. Occult circles flourished in St. Petersburg and Moscow, where they were attended by members of the aristocracy, artists and intellectuals. By this time, belief in witches had become much more widespread and accepted in Russia than it had before. This marked a turning point in attitudes toward witchcraft and ushered in an era of greater acceptance.

In modern times, there has been a revival of interest in Slavic paganism, particularly in Eastern Europe. It is considered a minority activity. Today, despite its dark past, many Russians view witchcraft with curiosity or even admiration due to its vibrant history and colourful customs.

Chapter 10: Witches in the Arts, Myths and Legends

The figure of the witch has long captivated the human imagination, appearing in various forms throughout history and across cultures. From ancient myths and legends to modern literature and film, the image of the witch has served as a symbol of power, femininity, and otherness. In this chapter, we will explore the nature of witches in fiction, the arts, and in myths and legends. Through an examination of various cultural expressions, visual arts, and popular culture, we will attempt to uncover the enduring appeal of the witch, and the rich cultural significance of this figure. In doing so we will also discover the different ways in which witches have been represented and interpreted over time.

A Source of Fascination

The creation and production of art have been fundamental aspects of human history, representing a new level of evolution and development in human society. Art has played a significant role in shaping our culture, beliefs, and values and has been used in many different ways throughout history. Through art, we can act out our emotions, both positive and negative, and explore what makes us feel powerful, vulnerable, and afraid. Art is a space where we can freely express ourselves, and it encourages us to explore the vast array of emotions that make us human.

Witches have long been a source of fascination in fiction and art, from ancient Greek playwrights such as Euripides to Shakespeare's Macbeth. These depictions range from classical portrayals of benevolent women healing the sick, to more sinister images of evil sorceresses casting spells for their own gain. In literature and art, witches embody fear—the fear of our own mortality and the unknown power that lies beyond it. Depictions of witches sometimes represent female autonomy—a woman who can challenge traditional gender roles and wield her own power without relying on others for approval or protection.

Many modern stories and films feature witches, including Harry Potter, The Wizard of Oz and The Craft to name but a few. These works explore the complexities of witchcraft in a variety of ways. These stories and films have helped drive the concept of witches and have made them become an important part of popular culture today. From Halloween costumes to video games, witches continue to be a source of fascination in literature, art and film.

Today's culture has embraced witches in an even bigger way through new media platforms such as Instagram, Pinterest, and YouTube. Here, witches can be seen taking on all sorts of roles—from inspiring art and fashion to teaching spells. These platforms have spawned a resurgence in "witchy culture", with an emphasis on female empowerment, self-care, and healing. This heightened interest in witches has opened the door for more diverse representations of them in modern media. It's a refreshing contrast to older portrayals and it has paved the way for a more inclusive storytelling about this timeless figure.

Witches in Fiction

Witches and sorcerers have always been important figures in fiction products. The idea of these figures being associated with evil coexist with other endearing characteristics. Witches are still favourite villains in horror movies, but they are also heroines. Examples include Hermione Granger in Harry Potter, Sabrina the Teenage Witch or Willow from Buffy the Vampire Slayer. Stereotypes change along with society, and now witches, or people with supernatural powers are not exclusively considered a danger to the rest of society. They are also portrayed as those that can save the rest of humankind.

The antiquated perception of witches as elderly, unattractive women has evolved, allowing for the inclusion of diverse representations of magical practitioners. In this category, it is possible to find Gandalf from The Lord of the Rings, or Albus Dumbledore from Harry Potter. These are portrayed as men (wizards) with powers they use for good. And then it is possible to find a young, beautiful witch that uses her powers to hurt others, like Bellatrix Lestrange, again from the Harry Potter series.

The world of traditional fairy tales, such as those compiled by the Brothers Grimm and Hans Christian Andersen, have long served as a cornerstone of our cultural heritage. These timeless stories often feature witches as central characters. They embody and reinforce specific social values and expectations placed upon women. By examining the roles and social mandates assigned to these figures, we can gain a deeper understanding of the underlying messages and cultural norms that these tales sought to communicate. In these tales, witches were evil and willing to harm. Besides this, they were ugly; they ate children, and they were jealous of other women.

Fiction reflects the social environment in which these stories were created. Historically, witches in fiction reinforce the existence of evil, and what can happen to people if they deviate their behaviour from the conventional accepted norm. The characters that embodied evil were used both to reproduce social stereotypes and to teach people about good and evil. It is believed that the origin of these stories—Sleeping Beauty, Little Red Riding Hood, Hansel and Gretel—were, in fact, based on real stories. They were communicated by word of mouth. Each speaker added components to the story and included extraordinary characters with supernatural powers. Was this an attempt, not only to deal with the grief of death and disappearance, but also a way to find an explanation?

The inexplicable, the uncontrollable, everything beyond human understanding has always caused fascination, but in particular, the emotion of fear. Fear is one of the intrinsic emotions of human nature. Like all the other emotions, it occurs in the brain and triggers a physical reaction that is essential for our survival. Fiction, in many ways, has helped to both provide fear, and at the same time, help to deal with its reality. One of the greatest horror story writers, Stephen King, once said this (McDaniel, 2021),

> I think of fear as a survival function, and in the stories that I write, the only thing that I've tried to do is provide people with nightmares which are really safe places to put those fears for a while (McDaniel, 2021).

In contemporary times, the concept of witches, witchcraft, and magic has evolved beyond their traditional associations with fear and dread. Instead, people are increasingly captivated by stories of magical beings wielding supernatural powers to save the world, as well as by witchcraft as a practice in its own right. This shift in perspective reflects a broader cultural transformation, where the allure of magic offers a tantalising window into worlds beyond our own, inviting us to reimagine the possibilities that lie just beyond the reach of the ordinary.

Witches in Theatre

Stories are the oldest form of fiction, even before cave paintings. They were produced and transmitted orally, generation after generation. In Ancient Greece, these stories had a great influence on their mythology, and the witch characters appeared in the first public expression of fiction: theatre. One of the earliest examples of this can be traced back to the ancient Greeks. They often included a supernatural element in their tragedies and comedies. For example, in Aristophanes' comedy

"The Birds" (414 BC), there is a reference to a witch character who prepared magical potions.

As the fear of witches and witchcraft intensified throughout Europe, playwrights began incorporating these themes into their works. During the Renaissance and the era of Elizabethan drama, witches became more prominent figures on the stage. One of the most famous examples of witches in theatre comes from the 17th century in William Shakespeare's tragedy "Macbeth". In this play, the predominant ideas about witches are crystallised in fiction. It famously opens with three witches who fortell Macbeth's rise to power, and his ultimate downfall. The witches are three powerful, dangerous, and untrustworthy matriarchs who have the power of divination. They also wield the power to influence the events they predict. Set at a time when witches were hunted and burned, these malicious and malevolent characters reflect the perception of witches in Shakespeare's time.

Following the Elizabethan era, the depiction of witches in theatre shifted as societal attitudes towards witchcraft evolved. During the Restoration period, playwrights often portrayed witches as comic figures, reflecting the diminishing belief in their powers. An example of this is Thomas Shadwell's play "The Lancashire Witches". In the 18th and 19th centuries, the Romantic movement saw a resurgence of interest in the supernatural, and witches once again appeared on stage as powerful, and often tragic figures. Goethe's "Faust" is a prime example, featuring a pact with the Devil and a visit to a witches' gathering. Faust's tragedy is often characterised as "titanism", as he attempts to transcend the constraints of human existence in pursuit of knowledge and experiences that are beyond the reach of humankind.

In more recent times, the portrayal of witches in theatre has become more varied and nuanced. Witches have been presented as sympathetic characters. This is seen in the Broadway musical "Wicked", which reimagines the Wicked Witch of the West from L. Frank Baum's "The Wonderful Wizard of Oz". Contemporary theatre today explores themes of female empowerment, liberation, sexuality, and social dynamics through its portrayal of witches.

Witches in Art

Throughout history, witches have featured prominently, not only in literature and theatre, but also in various other forms of art. As art often mirrors society and its prevailing ideologies, the portrayal of witches in these mediums provides valuable insight into the cultural contexts and beliefs of the time. By examining the evolution of witch portrayals in various art forms, we can gain a deeper understanding of the shifting perspectives on witchcraft throughout history and its impact on society's beliefs and values.

The role of witches and witchcraft images were used to expose the sinful and the dark side of human nature. They gave an ugly and scary face to evil, something people could be afraid of, and to make the abstract idea of evil visible and comprehensible.

There are many such examples of this. One of the earliest known depictions of witches in flight can be traced back to 1451, with an illustration created for a manuscript by French writer Martin Le Franc. Titled "Le Champion des Dames", the manuscript portrays Waldensian women as witches engaged in acts that were believed to involve the Devil. During this period, the Catholic Church viewed the Waldensians as a heretical sect, and they were subsequently persecuted as part of the growing witch craze. Le Franc's depiction of these witches played a pivotal role in shaping and disseminating the iconic image of witches that we recognise today. The illustration features women wearing voluminous dresses and, notably, shows them flying on broomsticks. This imagery not only solidified the association between witches and broomsticks but also contributed to the broader cultural narrative surrounding witchcraft and its practitioners.

In the following centuries, paintings included larger groups of witches. This was to increase the idea of danger: "Heretics, of course, were more frightening in large numbers, as they created a more significant threat to the status quo. If one witch was scary, a flying coven was downright terrifying" (Cohen, 2019). Most of the paintings representing witches came from Germany, the epicentre of the witch trials in early Modernity.

In the 17th century, allusions to witches in paintings included satanic scenes. One painting of note in this period belongs to the Italian painter Giovanni Benedetto Castiglione, who portrayed the sorceress Circe (see chapter 11) converting people into beasts (Cohen, 2019). Another is by Belgian painter Frans Francken the Younger. In his fantastical Bosch-like work, he depicts women gathered around a book of spells. Cohen (2019) interprets this as a message to—or from—society: "Beware a group of literate, independent women."

Figure 17: Frans Francken the Younger (1581–1642). Witches' Sabbath painting. Public domain, via Wikimedia Commons (https://commons.wikimedia.org/wiki/File:Frans_Francken_(II)_-_Witches%27_Sabbath.jpg)

When the witch craze ended, by the middle of the 18th century, witches became secondary characters in the paintings. The interest in them had decreased along with the fear they invoked. However, the Spanish painter, Goya, has two famous paintings featuring witches, painted at the end of the 18th century. These paintings are the "Witches' Sabbath" and "Witches' Flight". Both paintings are part of Goya's Black Paintings series. "Witches Sabbath" in particular reflects all the mediaeval conceptions of witches and their relationship with the Devil, their supernatural powers, and savage rituals of harming people. "Witches' Flight" is characteristic of Goya's later work, which often explored darker themes and employed a more sombre colour palette.

Figure 18: Witches Sabbath - Google Art Project. Francisco de Goya, Public domain, via Wikimedia Commons (https://commons.wikimedia.org/wiki/File:Francisco_de_Goya_y_Lucientes_-_Witches_Sabbath_-_Google_Art_Project.jpg)

The painting reflects his fascination with the supernatural and the irrational fears that gripped society during the era. An era when witchcraft and superstition played significant roles in shaping people's beliefs and behaviours.

Witches also started appearing in other forms of art such as sculpture and opera during this period. For example, Giacomo Meyerbeer's opera "The Witch" featured a witch character who uses her magic to protect her village from danger. In the 19th and 20th centuries, things changed dramatically. New conceptions about witchcraft in different social contexts resulted in positive images of witches. This still continues in their role as protagonists in many artistic expressions. With the waning of superstition and belief in witchcraft as real phenomenon, witches were being portrayed as benevolent guardians or protectors of nature. The idea that women were closer to nature than men was gaining momentum in Europe at this time, and art seemed to reflect this notion. Witches began to be seen as having magical powers that could help people and their communities rather than being wicked and baleful. The image of a witch became one of a wise, powerful woman. More recent paintings, like the one "The Magic Circle" by John William Waterhouse, show witches as young, attractive women. Although many symbols traditionally associated with witchcraft remain present in the artwork of this time, they are not used to express a threat but as symbols of protection and empowerment.

Today, witches have become part of popular culture and are being portrayed in art that is more light-hearted than ever before. This trend continues, with witches appearing in films, comic books, video games, and other forms of modern entertainment.

Myths and Legends of Witches

Morgan Le Fay

Morgan Le Fay is a powerful witch in Arthurian legend. In Thomas Malory's seminal work "Le Morte d'Arthur," Morgan Le Fay plays a pivotal role in the story of King Arthur's fall from grace. She was said to be the half-sister of King Arthur and had magical powers, including shape-shifting, healing, and prophesy. In some stories, she is portrayed as an evil rival to her brother, while in others she acts as his ally. Her name translates to "Sea Fairy" and she is often depicted living on the remote island of Avalon with her nine sisters.

In some interpretations, Morgan Le Fay plays a crucial role in the final events of King Arthur's life. It is said that she helps transport Arthur to the magical island of Avalon after he is mortally wounded in the Battle of Camlann. She also plays a part in his resurrection when she uses her powers to help him regain the full use of his limbs and return to Camelot. Morgan Le Fay is one of the most enduring characters of Arthurian legend, often serving as an interesting contrast to the more idealised images of King Arthur and The Knights of the Round Table. Her ambiguous nature serves to highlight some of the complexity and nuance found within these ancient stories. As time passes, Morgan's relevance appears to remain, with modern adaptations featuring her dramatic influence in film, literature and television.

Morgan Le Fay is commonly seen as a complex figure that operates somewhere between light and dark, good and evil. It is this duality that makes her so fascinating to readers and viewers across the ages. In some ways, she represents a side of humanity that often goes unacknowledged within more heroic tales—the darker aspects of our nature, our ability to make mistakes, and our capacity for both redemption and destruction.

Aradia

Aradia is a figure in Italian witchcraft, particularly in the tradition of Stregheria. She is said to be the daughter of the goddess Diana and the messenger sent by her mother to teach witchcraft to the peasantry. This was designed to aid them in their struggles against the Catholic Church and the wealthy landowning aristocracy in medieval Italy. She appears as the central figure in the book "Aradia, or the Gospel of the Witches," which was published in 1899 by the American folklorist Charles Godfrey Leland.

Leland claimed that the book was based on an ancient pre-Christian Italian text, which he claimed to have translated into English. The book presents a series of spells, invocations, and rituals that were supposedly used by Italian witches, along with a narrative about Aradia. Here she is presented as a goddess, or supernatural figure, who taught the witches their magic. Her story relates how she was sent by the gods to teach humans how to use magic and cast spells, as well as teaching them about nature and its spiritual power in everyday life. Aradia is also known for her strong sense of justice and advocacy for those who were oppressed or treated unfairly.

While the historical accuracy of Leland's claims has been disputed, "Aradia, or the Gospel of the Witches" became a significant influence on modern Wicca and other neo-pagan religions. The figure of Aradia, as presented in Leland's book, has been interpreted in a variety of ways by different neo-pagan groups, and has become associated with themes of female empowerment, rebellion against oppressive authority, and the use of magic to effect social change. She is still revered as a symbol of strength, courage and justice.

Circe

Circe was the daughter of the sun god Helios, and the Oceanid nymph, Perse. She was known as an enchantress who could turn people into animals with her powerful magic. Circe had a special potion that she used to transform unsuspecting visitors into wild beasts such as lions, wolves, and pigs. It is said that these unfortunate souls would remain in their animal form forever.

The most famous story involving Circe occurs when Odysseus visited her island home of Aeaea. He and his companions were lured there by the sweet smell of incense coming from her hallowed halls. When they arrived, Circe welcomed them warmly, but soon revealed her true intentions—to transform them all into animals. Fortunately for Odysseus, a god had given him a magical herb that protected him from Circe's evil spell. Despite her power, Odysseus was able to defeat her and force her to return his companions back to their human forms.

Figure 19: "Circe Offering the Cup to Ulysses". (Ulysses is the Roman name of Odysseus) (1891) by John William Waterhouse, Public domain, via Wikimedia Commons (https://commons.wikimedia.org/wiki/File:Circe_Offering_the_Cup_to_Odysseus.jpg)

The story of Circe is one of the most enduring myths in Greek mythology. It serves as a cautionary tale about the dangers of overconfidence and hubris—traits that can lead even the strongest mortals astray.

Chapter 11: Modern Day Witch Hunts

Advances in technology and communication have helped witchcraft to evolve in various ways. Witchcraft, as a practice and belief system, has long been influenced by its cultural and social context. With the advent of new technologies and communication methods, the scope and scale of this influence have expanded considerably. Online resources such as websites, blogs, e-books, and videos offer a wealth of information on the history, practices, and beliefs associated with witchcraft. Advances in communication have helped spread the knowledge and practice of witchcraft across cultural boundaries. As a result, modern witchcraft has become more diverse and eclectic, incorporating practices from various cultures and traditions. This has led to a broader understanding of witchcraft as a whole and has encouraged the development of new practices and approaches. While its exact form and practice may vary widely from one region to another, the underlying values and beliefs that motivate its practitioners remain remarkably consistent, emphasising a connection to nature, a reverence for life, and a belief in the power of the individual to shape their own destiny.

In the preceding chapters, we delved into the topic of witchcraft, examining it not as a mere manifestation of human imagination or engagement in the occult, but as an integral aspect of social life across cultures. We have observed its capacity to embody conflict, mirror societal divisions, and reveal the spiritual dimensions of human nature. Our exploration highlights the genuine desire for a connection beyond the material realm, one that transcends rational explanations. This unique quality renders witchcraft a significant subject matter, particularly for those with a rekindled interest in its practices.

In the 21st century, scientists continue to understand and explain witchcraft, sorcery, and magic. Witchcraft has been considered as a way to think and comprehend the world, but now, it is perceived as a new approach to understanding personhood and human consciousness. Magic expresses individuality, self-conceptualisation, and self-acknowledgement. Studies consider magic and witchcraft as new forms of participation, collective action, and social agency.

Witchcraft is examined as an aspect of contemporary life, serving as a means to challenge political authority, the state, and societal frameworks. For individuals residing in regions where modernity enforces its lifestyle, witchcraft provides a coping mechanism for navigating its relentless transformation. It serves as an outlet for the demands placed upon people. Meanwhile, in areas of the world that pursue a gradual, non-linear development on the periphery of modernity, witchcraft remains a tool for managing ongoing hardships and is used in an attempt to understand their cause.

Belief in Witchcraft Today

People all over the world, either in modern societies or in rural communities, continue to believe in magic and in witches. According to National Geographic, recent research affirms that, in Canada and the United Kingdom, for example, 13% of people believe in witches, and in the United States this range increases to 21% (Jones, 2022). From other sources however, these numbers reveal it is a marginal phenomenon and affirm that magic is perceived as mere entertainment.

Besides controversies about the scale of the phenomenon, the matter has two sides. On one side, there is the timeliness of popular interest in witchcraft and the increasing number of people believing and practising it. On the other, there is a renewed fear and persecution of witches. In the 21st century, witch hunts continue to exist and hundreds of people, particularly women, continue to die and suffer torture for being accused of its practice.

Modern Witch Hunts

In some political contexts, the concept of a witch hunt has been used to name the process of persecution of people with different political ideas. This alludes to the unjust or unfair motives and methods of the opponents by the established powers that feel threatened. In this context, the witch hunt is used as a metaphor. But in many societies, the idea of witchcraft in association with evil, and the persecution of those who are believed to practise it, is a very real phenomenon.

In our historical understanding, witch hunts are often predominantly linked to the period spanning roughly three centuries, from the middle of the 15th century to the middle of the 18th century. However, witch hunts did not simply vanish with the passage of time. In fact, even today, these persecutory practices continue to persist in various forms and contexts. For example, Müller and Sanderson (2020) point out that between 1960 and 2000, it is believed that upwards of 40,000 people were accused and murdered for practising witchcraft in Tanzania. According to this report, in certain countries (like Tanzania), this persecution is carried out by village authorities who judge and condemn with no more legitimacy than the witch trials of old. But the most striking and worrying fact is the social consensus that appears to support these informal trials.

Witchcraft practices also continue to exist in the developed world. It is not confined to rural traditional communities. In certain periods of our recent history, we have seen how social hysteria arises in western societies, like the satanic panic that took place in the United States in the 1980s.

Many international organisations declare that the number of witch trials continue to rise all over the world: "Women are still accused of practicing witchcraft each year. They are persecuted and even killed in organised witch hunts—especially in Africa but also in Southeast Asia and Latin America" (Müller & Sanderson, 2020). Accusations of witchcraft can be triggered for many reasons. For example, widespread illnesses, especially in places where people lack medical access and have low educational opportunities. The National Geographic highlights that "although belief in witchcraft is not limited to the developing world, witch trials occur more frequently there" (Jones, 2022). Just like it happened in the past, catastrophes and incomprehensible misfortune are attributed to witchcraft practices. Witches and witchcraft are still the scapegoats for social unrest.

Three centuries later, after the witch craze ceased, the brutality and injustice of the methods to prosecute and execute witches remain much the same. The accused are expelled from the community and obliged to live isolated lives. Individuals facing accusations must rely on their own resources and skills to survive, and this challenging situation extends to their families as well. Others are condemned to death by stoning or burning.

Another enduring pattern that has not only persisted but also intensified is that the majority of those identified as witches continue to be women. Additionally, in certain countries, numerous accusations are directed at children, many of whom are afflicted with HIV (Jones, 2022). We live in a world governed by the rationality of scientific knowledge. Powerful nations exist that assert their authority to influence and intervene at their discretion. However, women and children are still subjected to brutal violence, and even murder, for crimes they did not commit. These alleged offences lack any basis in existing legal systems and cannot be substantiated with evidence.

This troubling phenomenon highlights the underlying social, cultural, and gender inequalities that persist in many societies, even as the world at large embraces modernity and rational thought. It underscores the importance of addressing these injustices and structures that perpetuate such harmful practices.

The Situation in Africa

According to several international organisations—United Nations, World Health Organization, and Stepping Stones Nigeria, among others—Africa is the continent with more cases of witch hunts in the world (Jones, 2022).

Witchcraft has a long history in various parts of Africa, with its roots deeply embedded in traditional beliefs, cultural practices, and social structures. The term "witchcraft" encompasses a wide range of beliefs and practices across the continent. The reasons for its continued popularity and the problems associated with it can be attributed to several factors.

In many African societies, witchcraft is an integral part of traditional belief systems. These beliefs often provide explanations for misfortunes, illnesses, and other inexplicable events. As a result, witchcraft is sometimes used both as a coping mechanism and as a method for maintaining social order. Witchcraft accusations serve as a tool for settling disputes, managing competition, or expressing grievances in situations where formal legal recourse is limited or unavailable. In some cases, accusations of witchcraft are directed at vulnerable individuals as a means of seizing their property or resources.

In some areas of Africa, a limited access to education and awareness about scientific explanations for illnesses and natural events contribute to the persistence of witchcraft beliefs. Misunderstandings and fear further perpetuate these beliefs and practices. Some religious groups reinforce witchcraft beliefs, either by endorsing traditional practices or by condemning them as manifestations of evil—often exacerbating existing tensions and contributing to the problem further.

Africa's populations have been through different processes of subordination throughout history. Ancient empires conquered the territories of northern Africa, and these regions continued to be subdued by one empire after the other. In the 15th century, its coasts were visited and occupied by the European powers. They started by taking resources from Africa, and later, the people themselves. These people were kidnapped and sold as slaves. A few centuries later, they went for more and occupied all the territories, and made them colonies. From the end of the 19th century until the end of the Second World War, European powers dominated Africa. After the war, many independence movements started. The African people, who had lived under European oppression and within tribal communities, now faced the challenge of creating their own countries. These new nations had to work within systems that had been controlled by outsiders for centuries.

The presence of foreign powers not only conditioned the evolution of these societies, but also imposed a way of understanding the world. Mwashinga's research (2017) points out that:

> Witchcraft influences people's socioeconomic status in a direct way. This means that the state of the economy of a particular society is determined by the level of witchcraft

beliefs held, which in turn determines the socioeconomic status of families and individuals (p.3).

While some of these beliefs lead them to resort to asking witches or wizards for help, these beliefs also feed two types of fear—fear of bewitchment and fear of being accused of witchcraft.

The role of witchcraft in African societies is unique. Doctors still exist who play a role similar to the cunning folk in mediaeval Europe. They are qualified to provide medical attention, certifying their knowledge with diplomas conferred by local authorities (Kohnert, 2022). In addition to this, the author points out that witchcraft can have two different impacts—it represents either expressing rebellion against oppression or a tool to oppress. With the beginning of the decolonisation process, witchcraft has been used for political purposes: the new authorities impose and legitimise their powers by claiming to have supernatural traits. As Kohnert (2022) states,

> Some autocratic rulers use magic and witchcraft beliefs in rather offensive ways, either by attacking rivals directly using 'black magic' (e.g., poisoning, psycho-terror) or in using psychological warfare, by threatening potential voters and political opponents under the pretext of being able to see who is voting for them, and the subsequent threat of reacting accordingly (p. 8).

In general, witchcraft accusations in Africa work against the poor and deprived, and although witchcraft is believed to be practised by both genders, women are the more likely to be accused and condemned for witchcraft. In Nigeria, Congo, Ghana, Malawi, and South Africa, there are several cases of witch hunts having women, often poor women, and children as the most frequent victims. The accusations and procedures that include torture and murder are, so far, impossible to be controlled by the governments.

Mwashinga (2017) retrieves recent pieces of research to affirm that in 19 sub-Saharan countries, which concentrate 75% of Africa's population, witchcraft beliefs are held. This prevalence of witchcraft beliefs can be seen as a reflection of underlying cultural, historical, and spiritual factors that contribute to the unique characteristics of different African communities. As such, it is vital to approach the study of witchcraft in Africa with a recognition of the diverse experiences and contexts in which it is embedded.

Witchcraft remains a significant issue today in Africa due to its potential to cause social unrest, disrupt community harmony, and result in human rights abuses. Accusations of witchcraft have led to ostracism, violence, and even death for the accused. Additionally, the persistence of witchcraft beliefs has hindered development efforts by diverting attention and resources away from critical issues such as healthcare, education, and poverty reduction.

Other Parts of the World: Nepal and India

Witchcraft has been described as a social phenomenon, shaped by cultural and social nuances. Despite this, the situation of witch hunts is a worldwide occurrence with similar characteristics. For the purpose of this book and intending to illustrate the situation in other parts of the world, here we will discuss the conditions in Nepal and India, in southern Asia.

There is a common pattern between both countries: witchcraft and witch trials are determined by a profound gender bias. In the past, women had a special place in Asian mythology in Nepal and some parts of India. It is almost impossible to draw general conclusions about India because it is a large country. However, we shall refer to some regions to outline an example. Women were respected and cherished for their unique role within society as life givers, but after the Medieval Epoch when the Hindu religion became official, they began to lose all their rights. According to Paudel (2022),

> Women were regarded as inferior to man and were confined to the household as caretakers of their children and other family members and along with this their rights were also diminished in the name of family reputation and devotion. Thus, this belief gave rise to the male-dominated society and this patriarchal belief led the women to a most vulnerable situation (para. 2).

Women are the principal victims of accusations of witchcraft, which, for Paudel (2011), provides another means of violence and oppression by a patriarchal system. Witchcraft practices have always been a component of these cultures that consider practitioners having supernatural powers. But the historic and social evolution has shaped these people's minds to blame women for practising witchcraft with the ability to cause harm. Then, like in other contexts, social misfortune is attributed to witches who are usually widows, elderly women with low economic status, and especially those belonging to the lower castes.

Different pieces of scholarly research (Paudel, 2011; Atreya et al. 2021; Grigaitė, 2018) report hundreds of cases of witchcraft accusations in Nepal. These accusations are followed by public lynching by the members of the communities. Victims are tortured, beaten, and occasionally murdered. These communities are characterised by high levels of poverty and illiteracy, and a population with weak physical and mental health. These conditions lead people to believe that they are caused by witchcraft practices, and women who do not fit the norm are more likely to be found guilty (Atreya et al., 2021). Although the legal system protects women's rights, they are still the principal victims of violent attacks for witchcraft.

In India, the situation is quite similar. According to Biswas (2018), over 3,000 women have been killed in India for witchcraft in the last twenty years. Biswas asserts that, as seen in Nepal and numerous other nations, witch hunts are a prevalent occurrence in rural tribal communities. Significantly, these hunting practices are not carried out by official legal authorities, but rather emerge from within the communities themselves. The main causes for these witch hunts are social inequity and lack of primary services. When women are found guilty of witchcraft, they are tortured with all types of methods to inflict pain, and they are also publicly humiliated. "More than 2,500 Indians have been chased, tortured, and killed in such hunts between 2000 and 2016, according to India's National Crime Records Bureau" (Seema, 2018). Again, the principal victims are women belonging to the lowest social caste.

It seems to be clear that there is a close connection between the impoverished living conditions and illiteracy, and both the need and the fear of witchcraft. On one hand, witches are sometimes required to provide solutions to the domestic daily problems of the communities, and to give some kind of explanation for all the grief they suffer. On the other hand, it is so hard to cope with such misfortune and they lack further explanations, that all the bad that happens to them needs to be attributed to evil supernatural forces. When a society cannot find a way to guarantee survival and social peace, witches are the ones to blame. And with few exceptions, they happen to always be women.

Chapter 12: Modern Witchcraft Today

For many people, in the second half of the 20th century, new currents of witchcraft, Wicca, and Neo-paganism are the new ways to express spirituality in western societies. Many are reclaiming its ancient wisdom and seeking solace in its earth-based rituals. Today, witches proudly identify with their craft, finding empowerment and community in their practices and beliefs.

Wicca and Neo-paganism

Wicca and Neo-Paganism are terms often used interchangeably in modern spiritual discourse, but they represent distinct practices and belief systems. Both have emerged in response to a growing interest in alternative spiritual paths and a reconnection to ancient traditions.

Wicca is heavily influenced by pre-Christian European pagan practices, as well as esoteric traditions such as ceremonial magic, Freemasonry, and theosophy. Neo-Paganism, on the other hand, is an umbrella term that encompasses a wide range of contemporary spiritual movements that draw upon various ancient pagan religions and cultures. The 19th and early 20th centuries saw an occult revival, with several secret societies and magical orders gaining prominence. Groups like the "Hermetic Order of the Golden Dawn" and the "Ordo Templi Orientis" played a significant role in the development of modern magical and esoteric practices, which would later influence Neo-paganism. While some Neo-Pagan traditions may have emerged around the same time as Wicca, others have developed independently in different regions, inspired by diverse sources such as Celtic, Norse, Greek, or Egyptian beliefs.

For many, the traditional religions are considered anachronistic and insufficient to provide a system of beliefs in correspondence to the present changing world. In this context, these new models of beliefs are seen as ways to connect with the spiritual side and to connect with a metaphysical level. For many, these practices are not kept in secrecy anymore, and there is a greater acceptance of witches due to social media and pop culture. The portrayal of witches has undergone a significant transformation since the days of medieval Europe. While some continue to fear witches, for others, they have evolved into powerful symbols of empowerment, spiritual growth, and connection with nature. They embody a rich and complex history that challenges societal norms and expectations. Modern witches are ordinary folk who have a self-awareness of their condition: they can recognise their powers, and possess the extraordinary sensitivity that makes them different from the rest, and they search for others to create communities.

Neo-paganism proposes a return to nature and life in a better equilibrium with the environment. Modern witches identify themselves as practitioners that resist the system. They declare themselves "heretics" since they "commune with gods and spirits without the middleman of a priest or church telling us (them) we can't, and telling us what those gods and spirits are saying (…) which often turns out to be what said middleman wants it to be" (Aveytan, 2022). For these people witchcraft is a way to experience spirituality without having a hierarchical structure or a set of rules to follow. Somehow, in a world where everything is settled and calculated, witchcraft is a synonym for freedom.

Wicca, a branch of modern witchcraft, continues to attract followers and expand its community. Adherents of Wicca consider it a religion rooted in practices. They share a core set of beliefs. As an earth-centric or nature-based faith, Wicca emphasises the interconnection between humanity, nature, and the divine. The overarching belief is that the divine is present in humans and throughout nature. However, Wicca distinguishes itself from traditional religions by granting each practitioner the freedom to explore and express their faith and beliefs as they see fit.

Practitioners of both Neo-paganism and Wicca state that it provides a meaning and comfort to daily life. People who practise consider their rituals help them find certain order and security in a changing world that seems to be falling apart. Modern witchcraft has become an important part of the cultural narrative, representing freedom from traditional systems of belief and thought. It stands for a rejection of oppressive ideas and values imposed by religious or political authorities, offering instead an opportunity to explore spiritual connections that are more closely connected to nature and natural rhythms. This form of spirituality encourages exploration beyond the limits of conventional thinking, allowing individuals to express themselves in ways that defy traditional expectations. Through the practice of rituals and spells, practitioners are creating unique experiences tailored to their beliefs and needs.

The history of witchcraft is characterised by the diverse motivations and reasons that led numerous individuals to engage in its practice—to gain control over their lives in an unpredictable world. By using magical spells and rituals to summon good fortune, herbs to heal, and divination, witches had a variety of ways they could attempt to manipulate their environment. This same characterisation exists today.

Despite its prevalence, however, many have viewed Witchcraft with suspicion due to its association with dark forces and superstition. Despite this trepidation, Witchcraft has been practised for centuries and continues to be embraced by a growing number of individuals worldwide. As more people look for alternative sources of spiritual fulfilment and creative expression, Witchcraft provides an intriguing and powerful path to explore. Whether it be for controlling one's own destiny, healing ailments, or connecting with the divine, Witchcraft has become a source of empowerment and strength in many lives.

Witchcraft is often misunderstood, but its history reveals how its practitioners have sought to take back control in a chaotic world. As we continue to learn more about this fascinating practice, we can better understand why people have been drawn to it over the centuries. The remaining section of this chapter looks at such people.

Gerald Gardner

Gerald Gardner is an iconic figure in the world of witchcraft. He was a British occultist and witch who founded the Gardnerian tradition of Wicca, the modern-day practice of witchcraft. Gardner first encountered witchcraft during his travels in Europe, where he met members of a witches' coven practising their craft in secret. After returning to Britain, Gardner began to study and practise Witchcraft with the encouragement of his new friends. He wrote extensively on Witchcraft topics, creating rituals and teaching others about its principles and customs. His books served as foundational texts for those wishing to learn more about Witchcraft from a traditional European perspective. In addition to writing about Witchcraft, Gardner was also instrumental in drawing it forth out of the shadows and into mainstream society. He was one of the first to publicly admit to being a witch and held public rituals, which helped to spread awareness about Witchcraft throughout Britain. This, in turn, led to laws being passed that decriminalised the practice in 1951.

Today, Gardner's influence on modern-day Witchcraft is still felt. Many Witches acknowledge Gardner as an important figure in their faith and consider him a founding father of the craft. His writings remain popular sources for those interested in learning more about Witchcraft from a traditional standpoint, with his works providing detailed information on topics such as spells, magic, mythology and rituals.

Scott Cunningham

Scott Cunningham was a renowned author and practitioner of Wicca. He studied and practised the craft for over 25 years, during which he wrote numerous books about it. His two most popular works were "Wiccan Roots" and "Earth Power". In these books, Cunningham shared his vast knowledge of the craft, exploring its history, culture, rituals and beliefs. He also discussed how to use Earth power—energy from nature—to work magic. These books have become essential references for anyone interested in learning more about Wicca. They are considered classics in their field, providing readers with an authentic look at the craft's roots and practices. Cunningham was active in both teaching and practising the craft until his death in 1993.

Sybil Leek

Sybil Leek was an English witch who lived in the early 20th century. She was born in 1922 and was introduced to witchcraft at a young age by her grandmother. During her lifetime, she wrote several books about the practice of witchcraft, including The Complete Art of Witchcraft (1966) and Diary of a Witch (1968).

Leek's writings often focused on traditional Wicca beliefs as taught by Gerald Gardner. While practising during this time period, Sybil Leek also became an advocate for religious freedom and openly defended those accused of practising witchcraft. Her activism on this issue helped to create more acceptance of witchcraft and other alternative religions in the public eye.

Leek passed away in 1982, but her influence is still felt in the world of witchcraft today. Her writings have inspired generations of witches, and she continues to be remembered as a pioneer of modern Wicca. Despite the discrimination Sybil Leek experienced during her lifetime, she remained an outspoken advocate for religious freedom until her dying day.

Doreen Valiente

Doreen Valiente was a pioneering witch in the twentieth century, and is widely regarded as one of the most influential figures in modern Wicca. Her works "The Charge of the Goddess", "An ABC of Witchcraft", and "Witchcraft for Tomorrow" have been extremely influential in Wiccan culture and practice. She believed that witchcraft should be inclusive and accessible to everyone regardless of gender or race. Her writings emphasise respect for nature, self-empowerment, personal responsibility, and freedom from religious dogma. Valiente also spoke out against misogyny within the craft and sought to create an environment where all witches were free to express themselves without fear of judgement or persecution.

Alex Sanders

Alex Sanders was born in 1926 in the English town of Burnley. By his own admission, he had an interest in the occult from a young age and was started into Witchcraft by his grandmother at the age of seven. Throughout his life, he studied many forms of magic and paganism, eventually coming to form what would become known as Alexandrian Wicca in 1965.

Alexandrian Wicca is an eclectic mix of European folklore and ceremonial magick. Notable features include its strong emphasis on ritual, use of traditional Gardnerian elements such as the "Great Rite" and systemised hierarchy within covens. As founder of this tradition, Sanders became a well-respected figure among pagans and witches around the world. He wrote several books about his practices and beliefs, sharing his knowledge with followers and aspiring practitioners alike.

Although Sanders passed away in 1988, his legacy is still very much alive today. Alexandrian Wicca continues to be practised around the globe, offering an accessible way for many to connect with paganism and magic.

Stewart and Janet Farrar

Stewart and Janet Farrar were a well-known couple in the late twentieth century, especially in the Wiccan community. They wrote numerous books related to their practice, such as "Eight Sabbats for Witches", "The Witches' Way: Principles, Rituals and Beliefs of Modern Witchcraft" and "A Witches Bible Complete". This latter book was particularly significant because it offered an extensive description of rituals, magical practices, and beliefs related to Wicca. It also contained detailed instructions on how to perform spells and celebrate eight pagan festivals throughout the year. Through their work, Stewart and

Janet Farrar contributed majorly to the study of modern witchcraft and had a lasting impact on many generations of Wiccans. Many practitioners find inspiration from their work.

Dion Fortune

Dion Fortune was a renowned 20th century witch who used her magical knowledge to help those in need. She wrote books, founded the "Fraternity of the Inner Light", and developed an intuitive psychology based on esoteric principles that can apply to practical life.

Her most famous book, "The Sea Priestess", details her theories on how magical practices can be used to heal and transform people's lives. Dion Fortune also believed strongly in the power of set intentions and meditation as tools for spiritual awakening. Her teachings have inspired many modern practitioners of magick and spirituality and continue to influence countless individuals around the globe today.

Raymond Buckland

Raymond Buckland was an influential figure in the world of Wicca and modern witchcraft, often credited with introducing Wicca to the United States in the 1960s. Born in England, Buckland developed an early interest in the occult and spiritualism, which eventually led him to discover the writings of Gerald Gardner. In the early 1960s, Buckland corresponded with Gardner and eventually met him in person. Shortly thereafter, the Bucklands moved to the United States and founded the first American coven based on Gardnerian Wicca, known as the Long Island Coven.

Buckland's work and writings were instrumental in spreading Wicca across the United States. He authored numerous books on the subject, including the bestselling "Buckland's Complete Book of Witchcraft", which has become a standard text for many Wiccan practitioners.

Conclusion

This exploration of the history of witchcraft has taken us on a journey through time and across continents, from its ancient origins to the contemporary revival of the practice. We have examined the beliefs and practices that have come to define witchcraft, as well as the societal factors that have shaped its evolution.

Throughout history, witchcraft has been both revered and feared, a source of fascination and persecution. The witch trials in Europe and North America stand as a stark reminder of the hysteria and cruelty that can arise from ignorance and prejudice, while the more recent witch hunts in various parts of the world emphasise that such injustices are not entirely confined to the past. Despite centuries of persecution, witchcraft has endured and evolved. It has adapted to different cultural contexts and found new expressions in literature, art, and film. Through the portrayal of witches in fiction, the arts, and myths and legends, we have seen how these figures have often been used to explore and challenge societal norms and expectations.

It is a widely held belief that magic and witchcraft represent a precursor to the emergence of rational thinking and scientific knowledge, following a linear evolutionary path. This belief refers to the notion that human understanding of the world has evolved progressively, moving from primitive beliefs in magic and witchcraft to more sophisticated forms of thought grounded in reason and science. This perspective suggests that as human societies developed, they gradually abandoned superstitious practices and embraced rationality. However, this perspective has been critiqued for oversimplifying the complex and diverse ways in which different societies have engaged with, and understood the world. The transition from magical thinking to rational thought is not as clear-cut or universal as this linear view suggests. Many cultures, both ancient and modern, have blended or coexisted with elements of magic, religion, and science.

As we have seen, it is also a mistake to speak of witchcraft as a practice that happened in the past. Today, modern Western societies are experiencing a resurgence of movements that embrace various forms of witchcraft. For many in these societies, witchcraft offers an escape from a disenchanted world dominated by rationality and predictability, where spiritual experiences are scarce. In the past, witchcraft provided answers to the obscure, that reason couldn't explain; now, people turn to witchcraft as a means of stepping away from reason itself. Modern witchcraft represents the rebellion against rationality but also against the established ways to think and express individuality and spirituality. The system of ideas and beliefs supported by traditional science and religions seems to have failed to help people give sense to their lives.

As it has been explained through these pages, witchcraft has exposed social unrest and inequalities in different historical scenarios. Social differences and the targeting of vulnerable individuals often influenced who was accused of practicing witchcraft, which threatened the status quo. Typically, the poorest and lowest-ranking members of society were, and still are in some parts of the world, the victims of oppressive systems that labelled them as witches. The history of witchcraft is also the history of patriarchal and hierarchical societies that search and find scapegoats to prevail. Women, enslaved people, and the impoverished have always been, and still are, those that pay the price for social conflict dissipation.

The history of witchcraft reveals how human nature has not only problems coping with the unexpected and misfortune. It is hard to deal with those who are different, who see and experience the world from a different perspective. This history teaches that real evolution does not imply overcoming and leaving behind magical thinking or witchcraft, but embracing and respecting diversity. Witchcraft reminds us that there is a weak and sensitive part of human nature that deserves to be preserved and respected.

As we close the pages of this book, it is important to remember that the history of witchcraft is not only a story of persecution and misunderstanding but also one of resilience, adaptation, and, ultimately, the triumph of the human spirit. Through its enduring legacy, witchcraft has transcended the boundaries of time and geography, leaving an indelible mark on the tapestry of human history.

Delores E. Wren

Thank You

Writing a book is never an easy task. The process of researching and writing this book was no exception. But it was a labour of love, and I am grateful for the opportunity to share my passion for this fascinating subject with you.

I would like to extend a heartfelt thank you to all those who supported me during the writing of this book. Most of all, I would like to thank you, the reader, for taking the time to explore the history of witchcraft with me. I hope that this book has provided you with new insights and perspectives on this fascinating subject, and that it has sparked your curiosity and imagination.

Before I leave you, I wanted to ask just one tiny favour. If you enjoyed this book, I would be grateful if you could leave a review. This will take just a few minutes of your time. Feedback in the form of a review is invaluable. It helps to spread the word about this book and allows other readers to discover the rich history and cultural significance of witchcraft.

About the Author

Delores E. Wren is a passionate historian with a profound love for uncovering the mysteries and wonders of the past. Her fascination with history began in childhood, spending countless hours captivated by the stories of great civilisations and transformative events.

Over the years, Delores has cultivated a deep appreciation for history's ability to enrich our understanding of the human experience. Through her research and writing, Delores strives to shed light on the complex tapestry of human history, connecting the dots and uncovering the intricate patterns that define our collective heritage.

References

The study of witchcraft is a journey of continuous discovery, and I hope that this book has ignited your curiosity and inspired you to explore this captivating subject further.

Witchcraft is a vast subject, encompassing an array of beliefs, practices, and historical events. Although it is impossible to capture every nuance or aspect of witchcraft within the confines of a single book, this work has endeavoured to provide a comprehensive overview of the subject, but it is by no means exhaustive. There are countless other stories and perspectives to be explored. Indeed, new research continues to shed light on the myriad dimensions of witchcraft. As such, this book should be seen as a starting point for understanding the rich and complex history of witchcraft. For those seeking to delve further into the subject, there are numerous resources, academic studies, and accounts available that will provide additional insight and context.

The following resources and references were used during the research and creation of this book and make an excellent starting point for further research of your own.

Atreya, A., Aryal, S., & Nepal, S. (2021) *Accusations of witchcraft: A form of violence against women in Nepal Medicine, Science, and the Law* 61(2) www.researchgate.net/publication/349632929_Accusations_of_witchcraft_A_form_of_violence_against_women_in_Nepal

Avetyan, M., Huffman, R., Solis, L., Ced, G., and Weiss, J. (2022) *Witchcraft. Witchcraft – Beliefs: An Open Invitation to the Anthropology of Magic,*

Witchcraft, and Religion.
oer.pressbooks.pub/beliefs/chapter/witchcraft/

Bado-Fralick, N. (n.d.) *Mapping the Wiccan Ritual Landscape: Circles of Transformation.* core.ac.uk/download/pdf/213811084.pdf

Bailey, M. (2006) *The Meanings of Magic. Magic, Ritual, and Witchcraft.* 1(1) muse.jhu.edu/pub/56/article/236416

Ben-Yehuda, N. (1980) *The European Witch Craze of the 14th to 17th Centuries: A Sociologist's Perspective.* American Journal of Sociology. 86(1) 1-31 www.jstor.org/stable/2778849?read-now=1&seq=24#page_scan_tab_contents

Berger, H. (2005) *Witchcraft and Magic: Contemporary North America.* University of Pennsylvania Press. www.jstor.org/stable/j.ctt3fh7kf

Berger, H. (2021) *What is Wicca? An expert on modern witchcraft explains.* Brandeis Now. www.brandeis.edu/now/2021/september/wicca-berger-conversation.html

Beyer, C. (2019) *The Difference Between Magic and Magick.* Learn Religions. www.learnreligions.com/magic-and-magick-95856

Biswas, A.K. (2018) *Witch hunts in the 21st century: A serious challenge to the empowerment of rural tribal women in India.* Brolly. Journal of Social Sciences 1 (2) www.researchgate.net/publication/344932860_WITCH-HUNTS_IN_THE_21_ST_CENTURY_A_SERIOUS_CHALLENGE_TO_THE_EMPOWERMENT_OF_RURAL_TRIBAL_WOMEN_IN_INDIA

Blécourt, W. and Davies, O. (2020) *Witchcraft Continued.* Manchester University Press. manchesteropenhive.com/view/9781526137975/9781526137975.00013.xml

Blumberg, J. (2022) *A Brief History of the Salem Witch Trials*. Smithsonian. www.smithsonianmag.com/history/a-brief-history-of-the-salem-witch-trials-175162489/

Breslaw, E. (2000) *Witches of the Atlantic world: a historical reader & primary sourcebook*. New York University Press. wellcomecollection.org/works/ev86qamb

Brethauer, A. (n.d.) *Grimoire vs Book of Shadows: Discover Their Fascinating Origins*. The Peculiar Brunette. thepeculiarbrunette.com/history-and-origins-of-grimoires-book-of-shadows/

Britannica, The Editors of Encyclopaedia. (2022) *Amulet*. Encyclopaedia Britannica. britannica.com/topic/amulet.

Britannica, The Editors of Encyclopaedia (2022) *Satanism*. Encyclopaedia Britannica. britannica.com/topic/Satanism. Accessed 6 December 2022.

Britannica, The Editors of Encyclopaedia (2022) *Necromancy*. Encyclopaedia Britannica. britannica.com/topic/necromancy

Broedel, H.P. (2003) *The Malleus Maleficarum and the construction of witchcraft*. Manchester University Press. library.oapen.org/bitstream/handle/20.500.12657/35002/341393.pdf?sequence=1&isAllowed=y

Clifton, C. (2019) *Review of "The Witch: A History of Fear, from Ancient Times to The Present," by Ronald Hutton*. The Pomegranate: The International Journal of Pagan Studies. academia.edu/41364349/Review_of_The_Witch_A_History_of_Fear_from_Ancient_Times_to_The_Present_by_Ronald_Hutton

Cohen, A. (2019) *Why artists have been enchanted by witchcraft for centuries*. Artsy. artsy.net/article/alina-cohen-artists-enchanted-witchcraft-centuries

Cornell University Press (n.d.) *Witchcraft and Magic in Russian and Ukrainian Lands before 1900* cornellpress.cornell.edu/witchcraft-and-magic-in-russian-and-ukrainian-lands-before-1900/

Czarina (2022) *Warlock vs Wizard: What's The Difference?* Facts.net. facts.net/warlock-vs-wizard/

Dashu, M. (2012) *Another View of the Witch Hunts.* Pomegranate The International Journal of Pagan Studies 13(9):30-43 www.researchgate.net/publication/276914329_Another_View_of_the_Witch_Hunts

Deyrmenjian, M. (2020) *Pope Innocent VIII (1484-1492) and the Summis desiderantes affectibus.* PDXScholar. pdxscholar.library.pdx.edu/cgi/viewcontent.cgi?article=1001&context=mmft_malleus

Duni, M. (2020) *Witchcraft and witch hunting in late medieval and early modern Italy.* academia.edu/44442040/Witchcraft_and_witch_hunting_in_late_medieval_and_early_modern_Italy

Ellis, E. (2021) *The World's Most Magical Plants.* Oak Spring Garden Foundation. www.osgf.org/blog/2021/10/25/the-most-magical-plants

Farrell, D., Zunner, A. & Aveytan, M. (n.d.) *Witchcraft – Beliefs: An Open Invitation to the Anthropology of Magic, Witchcraft, and Religion.* PressBooks.

5 Real Witches in History - Biography (2014) Biography (Bio.) biography.com/news/real-witches-in-history

Folk magic and witchcraft | What's the difference (2016) Cailleach's Herbarium. cailleachs-herbarium.com/2016/05/folk-magic-witchcraft-whats-the-difference/

Ford, M., Hakl, H., and Hanegraaff, W. (n.d.) *Luciferianism.* Encyclopedia.pub. encyclopedia.pub/entry/37468

Gaspar, L. (2013) Talismãs e amuletos. Pesquisa Escolar Online, Joaquim Nabuco Foundation, Recife. basilio.fundaj.gov.br/pesquisaescolar_en/index.php?option=com_content&id=1310:talismans-amulets

Giralt, S. (2017) *Medieval necromancy, the art of controlling demons.* Sciencia.cat. www.sciencia.cat/temes/medieval-necromancy-art-controlling-demons

Grigaitė, U. (2018) *Witchcraft Accusation and Persecution of Women in Nepal.* vbplatforma.org/uploaded_files/articles/Nepal%20WAP%20Report.pdf

Gunn, R. (2003) *Witchcraft in Medieval Scotland.* Skye-Net. skyelander.orgfree.com/witch1.html

Gwynn, J. (n.d.). *Witchcraft in 17th-century Flintshire.* National Library of Wales. library.wales/discover-learn/digital-exhibitions/archives/witchcraft-court-of-great-sessions-rec/witchcraft-in-17th-century-flintshire

Hammer, J. (2022) *Spain's Centuries-Long Witch Hunt Killed 700 Women.* Smithsonian Magazine. www.smithsonianmag.com/history/spain-centuries-long-witch-hunt-killed-700-women-180981018/

Hamilton, B. & Peters, E. (2022) *Inquisition.* Encyclopaedia Britannica. britannica.com/topic/inquisition

Harper, D. (n.d.). *Etymology of potion.* Online Etymology Dictionary. etymonline.com/word/potion

Harris, V. (2020) *Witches on Surfboards: How Witch Media Has Ridden the Waves of Feminism.* Cardinal Compositions. (4):39-43. ir.library.louisville.edu/cgi/viewcontent.cgi?article=1007&context=cardcomp

Hartigan-O'Connor, E. (2020) *Witchcraft in the Atlantic World.* www.oxfordbibliographies.com/view/document/obo-9780199730414/obo-9780199730414-0145.xml

Hillis, E. (n.d.) *The unique concept of the Witch and the Witch trials in early modern England. Luther College.* The University of Regina. luthercollege.edu/university/academics/impetus/spring-2011/the-unique-concept-of-the-witch-and-the-witch-trials-in-early-modern-england/

https://www.facebook.com/thoughtcodotcom. (2013). The Malleus Maleficarum Was a Medieval Witch Hunter Handbook. ThoughtCo. https://www.thoughtco.com/malleus-maleficarum-witch-document-3530785

Hunt, C. (2022) *The Great European witch hunt in Elizabethan England and Jacobean Scotland.* repository.arizona.edu/bitstream/handle/10150/297652/azu_etd_mr_2013_0110_sip1_m.pdf?sequence=1

Hutton, R. (2006) *Shamanism: Mapping the Boundaries. Magic, Ritual, and Witchcraft.* University of Pennsylvania Press. Vol. 1, No 2, pp. 209-213. muse.jhu.edu/article/236470/pdf

Hutton, R. (2014) *The Wild Hunt and the Witches' Sabbath Folklore.* University of Bristol - Explore Bristol Research. 125(2):161-178. research-information.bris.ac.uk/ws/files/38162196/WildHunt_first_edit.pdf

Hutton, R. (2017) *Ronald Hutton on the Witch.* History Extra. The official website for BBC History Magazine and BBC History Revealed. historyextra.com/period/medieval/ronald-hutton-on-the-witch/

Hutton, R. (2017) *Five Characteristics of a Witch- an extract by Ronald Hutton.* Yales Books. yalebooksblog.co.uk/2017/07/31/five-characteristics-of-a-witch-an-extract-by-ronald-hutton/

Inquisition | Roman Catholicism. (2019). In Encyclopædia Britannica. https://www.britannica.com/topic/inquisition

Johns, C. (2022) *Witch Trials in the 21st Century.* National Geographic Society. education.nationalgeographic.org/resource/witch-trials-21st-century

Johnson, S. (2021) *Book of Shadows vs Grimoire | What's the Difference?* Arcane Alchemy. arcane-alchemy.com/blog/2021/1/6/book-of-shadows-vs-grimoire-whats-the-difference

Kaelber, L. (n.d.) uvm.edu/~lkaelber/teaching/WiccaSatan.docx

Kessler, P. & Dawson, E. (n.d.) *Kingdoms of the Germanic Tribes - Germanic Tribes (Teutons)* The History Files www.historyfiles.co.uk/KingListsEurope/BarbarianGermanics.htm (Ch 6)

King, G. (2017) *Peering into the scrying mirror at the Museum of Witchcraft.* Museum Crush. museumcrush.org/peering-into-the-scrying-mirror-at-the-museum-of-witchcraft/

Kibor, E. (2006) *Witchcraft and Sorcery: A biblical perspective with implications for church ministry.* African Journal of Evangelical Theology. biblicalstudies.org.uk/pdf/ajet/25-2_151.pdf

Kirk, J. and Williams, H. (2010) Futhark. *International Journal of Runic Studies. Vol. I.* uu.diva-portal.org/smash/get/diva2:381122/FULLTEXT01.pdf

Kivelson, V. (2022) *Where the witches were men: A historian explains what magic looked like in early modern Russia.* The Conversation. theconversation.com/where-the-witches-were-men-a-historian-explains-what-magic-looked-like-in-early-modern-russia-182392

Kohnert, D. (2022). *Magic and Witchcraft: Implications for democratization and poverty-alleviating aid in Africa.* SSOAR. ssoar.info/ssoar/bitstream/handle/document/55638.2/ssoar-2022-kohnert-Magic_and_Witchcraft_Implications_for.pdf?sequence=1&isAllowed=y&lnkname=ssoar-2022-kohnert-Magic_and_Witchcraft_Implications_for.pdf

Knutsen, G. (2002) *Where did the witches go? Spanish witches after their trials.* academia.edu/20230168/Where_did_the_witches_go_Spanish_witches_after_their_trials

Lambert, T. (2022) *The Background to the Witch Trials.* Local Histories. localhistories.org/a-history-of-the-witch-trials-in-europe/

Litinas, M. (2016) *Perceptions of Magic in Early Modern Orthodoxy.* Universiteit Leiden. academia.edu/37480671/Perceptions_of_Magic_in_Early_Modern_Orthodoxy

Lynn, M. (2018) *Magic and Witchcraft in Early Modern Europe.* The Newberry. Essay Collection. dcc.newberry.org/?p=14415

McDaniel, C.J. (2021) *Stephen King on Writing Quotes: A Must-Read Collection.* Adazing. adazing.com/stephen-king-on-writing-quotes/

Magazine, S., & Hammer, J. (n.d.). *Spain's Centuries-Long Witch Hunt Killed 700 Women. Smithsonian Magazine.* https://www.smithsonianmag.com/history/spain-centuries-long-witch-hant-killed-700-women-180981018/

Magliocco, S. (2009) *In Search of the Roots of Stregheria.* Oral History, Oral Culture, and Italian Americans. academia.edu/47503101/In_Search_of_the_Roots_of_Stregheria

Magliocco, S. (2014) *New Age and Neopagan Magic.* academia.edu/11296663/New_Age_and_Neopagan_Magic

Magliocco, S. (2018) *Witchcraft, healing and vernacular magic in Italy. Witchcraft Continued.* Research Gate. www.researchgate.net/publication/327127917_Witchcraft_healing_and_vernacular_magic_in_Italy

Marr, C. (2022) *Sigils and Runes.* Cathryn Marr Author. cathrynmarr.com/2022/06/30/join-us-at-the-romance-retreat-in-riverside/

Martinelli, S.S. (2020) *Botanical Magic: Plants in Myth and Folklore*. Three Leaf Farm. threeleaffarm.com/blog/botanical-magic-plants-in-myth-and-folklore

Meet the Slavs (2021) *Slavic Paganism: History and Rituals*. meettheslavs.com/slavic-paganism/

Mederos. (2020) *Women or Witches? Why Women Were the Target of the Malleus Maleficarum*. pdxscholar.library.pdx.edu/mmft_malleus/2/

Melton, G. (2022) *Church of Satan*. American movement. Encyclopaedia Britannica. britannica.com/topic/Church-of-Satan

Merriam-Webster (n.d.) *Heresy*. merriam-webster.com/dictionary/heresy

Merriam-Webster (n.d.) *Necromancy*. www.merriam-webster.com/dictionary/necromancy

Merriam-Webster (n.d.) *Ritual*. merriam-webster.com/dictionary/ritual

Merriam-Webster (n.d.) *Sorcery*. merriam-webster.com/dictionary/sorcery

Merriam-Webster (n.d.) *Witchcraft*. merriam-webster.com/dictionary/witchcraft

Mesaki, S. (1995) *The Evolution and Essence of Witchcraft in Pre-Colonial African Societies*. Transafrican Journal of History. 24:162-177. jstor.org/stable/24328661?read-now=1&seq=1#page_scan_tab_contents

Moro, P. (2019) *Witchcraft, Sorcery, and Magic*. Wiley Online Library. onlinelibrary.wiley.com/doi/full/10.1002/9781118924396.wbiea1915

Mount, T. (2015) *Snail poultices and blood potions: 9 weird medieval medicines*. History Extra. The official website for BBC History Magazine and BBC History Revealed. historyextra.com/period/medieval/9-weird-medieval-medicines/

Müller, J. (1998) *Love Potions and the Ointment of Witches: Historical Aspects of the Nightshade Alkaloids.* Journal of toxicology. Clinical toxicology 36(6): 617-27.
researchgate.net/publication/13509181_Love_Potions_and_the_Ointment_of_Witches_Historical_Aspects_of_the_Nightshade_Alkaloids

Muller, C. & Sanderson, S. (2020) *Witch hunts: A global problem in the 21st century.* DW. dw.com/en/witch-hunts-a-global-problem-in-the-21st-century/a-54495289

Mwashinga, C. (2017) *Relationship between Social and Economic Status and Witchcraft in Africa.* Andrews University digitalcommons.andrews.edu/cgi/viewcontent.cgi?article=1355&context=jams

NEPAL: Witchcraft as a Superstition and a form of violence against women in Nepal. (n.d.). Asian Human Rights Commission. Retrieved May 6, 2023, from http://www.humanrights.asia/opinions/AHRC-ETC-056-2011/

Newcombe, R. (n.d) *Rune Guide - An Introduction to using the Runes.* Holistic Shop. holisticshop.co.uk/articles/guide-runes

Nitschke, L. (2022) *European Witch-Hunting (A Brief History)* The Collector. thecollector.com/european-witch-hunting/

Notestein, W. (2014) *A History of Witchcraft in England from 1558 To 1718.* Global Grey. www.globalgreyebooks.com/history-of-witchcraft-ebook.htmlO'Gieblyn, M. (2019) Objects of Despair: Mirrors. The Paris Review. theparisreview.org/blog/2019/03/04/objects-of-despair-mirrors/

Parish, H. (2019) *Paltrie Vermin, Cats, Mise, Toads, and Weasels: Witches, Familiars, and Human-Animal Interactions in the English Witch Trials.* Witchcraft, Demonology, and Magic. mdpi.com/books/pdfdownload/book/2289

Paudel, S. (2011) NEPAL: *Witchcraft as a Superstition and a form of violence against women in Nepal.* Asian Human Rights Commission. humanrights.asia/opinions/AHRC-ETC-056-2011/

Pearson, J. (2000) *Religion and the Return of Magic: Wicca as Esoteric Spirituality.* eprints.lancs.ac.uk/id/eprint/133457/1/11003543.pdf

Priest, R. (2012) *On the Meaning of the Words "Witch," "Witchcraft," and "Sorcery".* Henry Center. On the Meaning of the Words "Witch," "Witchcraft," and "Sorcery" | Carl F. H. Henry Center for Theological Understanding (tiu.edu)

Polkes, A., Bassett, A., and Laveau M. (2019) *9 Famous Witches Throughout History.* The Lineup. the-line-up.com/6-famous-witches

Redden, A. (2013) *The Problem of Witchcraft, Slavery and Jesuits in Seventeenth-century* New Granada. livrepository.liverpool.ac.uk/3000809/1/Redden-WitchraftSlaveryJesuits-finalcorrected-BHS90_2_08.pdf

Rosen, M. (2017) *A Feminist Perspective on the History of Women as Witches.* SOAR. soar.suny.edu/bitstream/handle/20.500.12648/2749/dissentingvoices/vol6/iss1/5/fulltext%20%281%29.pdf?sequence=1&isAllowed=y

Satanism (2019) History.com. history.com/topics/1960s/satanism

Savage, W. (2017) *"Cunning Folk": Witchcraft, Healing and Superstition.* Pen and Pension. penandpension.com/2017/11/29/cunning-folk-witchcraft-healing-and-superstition/

Schoonmaker, J. (2015) *The Witches' Sabbath.* Manchester Historian. manchesterhistorian.com/2015/the-witches-sabbath/

Sedgwick, I. (2020) *Spells & Scrying: Mirrors in Magic, Mythology & Folklore.* Icy Sedgwick. icysedgwick.com/mirrors-spells/

Seema, Y. (2018) *Witch Hunts Today: Abuse of Women, Superstition and Murder Collide in India.* Scientific American. scientificamerican.com/article/witch-hunts-today-abuse-of-women-superstition-and-murder-collide-in-india/

Shade, P. (2022) *The Supernatural Side of Plants. Cornell Botanic Gardens.* Cornell University. cornellbotanicgardens.org/the-supernatural-side-of-plants-2/

Shamanism, Witchcraft, and Magic: Foreword (2006) Magic, Ritual, and Witchcraft. University of Pennsylvania Press. 1(2):207-208. muse.jhu.edu/article/236469/pdf

Shewan, D. (2017) *Conviction of Things Not Seen: The Uniquely American Myth of Satanic Cults.* Pacific Standard. psmag.com/social-justice/make-a-cross-with-your-fingers-its-the-satanic-panic

Shukla, A. (2021) *Spelling it Out: Accepting and Recontextualizing Traditional East Slavic Understandings of Nature and Maladies as Expressed in Zagovory from Polesia.* swarthmore.edu/sites/default/files/assets/images/linguistics/SWAT%20Anatole%20Shukla.pdf

Singh, M. (2020) *The Foundations of Shamanism and Witchcraft.* Doctoral dissertation. Harvard University, Graduate School of Arts & Sciences. dash.harvard.edu/bitstream/handle/1/37365897/SINGH-DISSERTATION-2020.pdf?sequence=1&isAllowed=y

Singh, M. (2020) *Magic, explanations, and evil. On the origins and design of witches and sorcerers.* Research Gate. www.researchgate.net/publication/349617609_Magic_Explanations_and_Evil_The_Origins_and_Design_of_Witches_and_Sorcerers

Sluhovsky, M. (2918) *Satanism: A Social History, written by Massimo Introvigne.* Journal of Jesuit Studies, 5(1):181-182.

brill.com/view/journals/jjs/5/1/article-p181_181.xml?language=en

Smith, G. (2017) *Witchcraft law up to the Salem witchcraft trials of 1692.* Massachusetts Government. mass.gov/news/witchcraft-law-up-to-the-salem-witchcraft-trials-of-1692

Smith, Z. (2016) *The Novice's Grimoire: Scrying.* Catalyst Magazine. catalystmagazine.net/the-novices-grimoire-scrying/

Spajić, A. (2020) *Women's Empowerment in Neopaganism.* Uppsala University. uu.diva-portal.org/smash/get/diva2:1439053/FULLTEXT01.pdf

Stavynska, Y. (2021) *Unfamiliar Familiars: Historical Witches' Magical Helpers.* blogs.uoregon.edu blogs.uoregon.edu/enchanted/2021/12/02/unfamiliar-familiars-historical-witches-magical-helpers/

Starling, M. (2022) *An Introduction to Welsh Witchcraft.* Llewellyn. llewellyn.com/journal/article/2994

Stregheria. (2022, May 12). Wikipedia. https://en.wikipedia.org/wiki/Stregheria

Stringer, M. (2015) *A War on Women? The Malleus Maleficarum and the Witch-Hunts in Early Modern Europe.* thesis.honors.olemiss.edu/459/1/Malleus%20Maleficarum%20Final.pdf

Tavuzzi, M. (2007) *Renaissance Inquisitors: Dominican Inquisitors and Inquisitorial Districts in Northern Italy, 1474-1527.* Brill. www.jstor.org/stable/10.1353/ren.2008.0106

The Pluralism Project (n.d) *Magick.* Harvard University. pluralism.org/magick

Toon, F. (2021) *'We are the granddaughters of the witches you couldn't burn'.* Penguin. penguin.co.uk/articles/2021/03/francine-toon-pine-inner-witch-violence-against-women

Trammell, S. (2020) *Witch-Media: A Lens for Understanding Female Empowerment*. Baylor University. baylor-ir.tdl.org/bitstream/handle/2104/10943/Witch-Media%20A%20Lens%20for%20Understanding%20Female%20Empowerment.pdf?sequence=5

Twigg, B. (2021) *To Be a Wits: An Exploration of Witchcraft and Gender in Early Modern Wales*. Open Research Online. oro.open.ac.uk/78851/1/TWIGG_A329_RVOR.pdf

Vann, R. (2022) *Society of Friends*. Encyclopaedia Britannica. britannica.com/topic/Society-of-Friends

Walker, W. and Berryman, J. (2018) *Ritual Closure: Rites De Passage and Apotropaic Magic in an Animate World*. J Archaeol Method Theory. 1-46. ncbi.nlm.nih.gov/pmc/articles/PMC9206089/

Waterman, H. (2017) *Herbs & Verbs: How to Do Witchcraft for Real*. daily.jstor.org. daily.jstor.org/herbs-verbs-how-to-do-witchcraft-for-real/

Why are cats associated with witches (2015) Animal Friends. animalfriends.co.uk/cat/cat-blog/why-are-cats-associated-with-witches

Witchcraft law up to the Salem witchcraft trials of 1692 | Mass.gov. (n.d.). Www.mass.gov.https://www.mass.gov/news/witchcraft-law-up-to-the-salem-witchcraft-trials-of-1692

Wikipedia Contributors. (2019, April 28). *Matthew Hopkins*. Wikipedia; Wikimedia Foundation. https://en.wikipedia.org/wiki/Matthew_Hopkins

Wilby, E. (2013). *Burchard's strigae, the Witches' Sabbath, and Shamanistic Cannibalism in Early Modern Europe*. Magic, Ritual, and Witchcraft, 8(1), 18–49. doi.org/10.1353/MRW.2013.0010

Wigington, P. (2019) *What is Scrying?* Learn Religions. learnreligions.com/what-is-scrying-2561865

Wigington, P. (2013) *What is a Pagan Animal Familiar? Learn Religions.* learnreligions.com/what-is-an-animal-familiar-2562343

Witchcraft, Women & the Healing Arts in the Early Modern Period: Wise-Women & Cunning Folk Healers (2022) Research Guides. guides.library.uab.edu/c.php?g=1048546&p=7609198

Zguta, R. (1977) *Witchcraft Trials in Seventeenth-Century Russia.* The American Historical Review 82(5), 1187-1207 jstor.org/stable/1856344?read-now=1&seq=21#page_scan_tab_contents

Printed in Great Britain
by Amazon